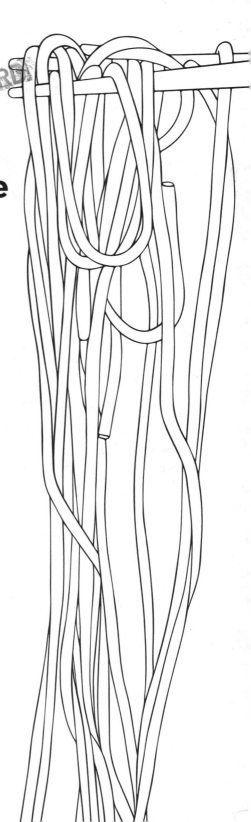

Start Your Business on a Ramen Noodle Budget

12 Lessons on Becoming a Young Entrepreneur When You Are Broke

D1441347

Felecia Hatcher-Pearson

 **PETERSON'S**®

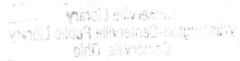

PETERSON'S®

About Peterson's®

Peterson's®, a Nelnet company, has been your trusted educational publisher for over 50 years. It's a milestone we're quite proud of, as we continue to offer the most accurate, dependable, high-quality education content in the field, providing you with everything you need to succeed. No matter where you are on your academic or professional path, you can rely on Peterson's for its books, online information, expert test-prep tools, the most up-to-date education exploration data, and the highest quality career success resources—everything you need to achieve your educational goals. For our complete line of products, visit **www.petersons.com**.

Previously published as *How to Start a Business on a Ramen Noodle Budget: 12 Super Awesome Lessons On Becoming A Young Entrepreneur When You Are Broke*. Copyright 2009.

For more information, contact Peterson's, 3 Columbia Circle, Albany, NY 12203; 800-338-3282 Ext. 54229; or find us online at www.petersons.com.

ISBN: 978-0-7689-4079-4

Printed in the United States of America

10 9 8 7 6 5 4 3 2 1 18 17 16

First Edition

This book is dedicated to my daughter Ori.

Table of Contents

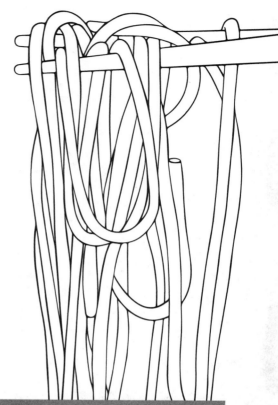

Chapter 1

Your Ideas Are Worthless!

I EAT
ramen noodles
NOW SO THAT
I CAN EAT
Lobster
LATER.
~HERBY FABIUS

Chapter 1
Your Ideas Are Worthless!

Your ideas are worthless! Yep, that's right, I said it! Your ideas mean absolutely nothing without a strategic action plan and execution! Think of how many ideas you come up with during the day or in a week. Many of them never even reach paper because we think that we cannot move forward until we raise money. Too often, we are more obsessed with the idea of dreaming big and accomplishing the unimaginable than actually doing the work.

In order to build traction with your big idea, it needs to be practical. Being practical can make it easier to start a business on a Ramen Noodle budget. I'm a big advocate of starting small but constantly thinking big. You can start a business now, with all of the resources you currently have and less than 1% of what you think you need to accomplish your grandiose vision. The key is to start where you are with what you have by building a trial product, just to get yourself in the game. This will put you way ahead of most, because you have actually started—while others are waiting for the finish line to appear magically at the starting line.

> Ideas are worthless! Execution is absolutely everything.

For example, let's say you have a dream of starting your own university that will allow free access to higher education for people in third-world countries. You envision it will change the dynamics of education worldwide, with thousands of students, campuses all over the world, and expensive technology. However, instead of waiting for that perfect day and going into a panic attack wondering how you will fund it, you start by teaching a Udemy.com class this weekend. The technology that is available to us today makes it easier than ever to start a business on a Ramen Noodle budget. You can set up a class today. Tap into your social networks, and find people who will pay to learn from your expertise. All you need is a computer, internet access, and the will to be patient and execute. You will be in business, and it can grow from there.

When we first started Feverish, we purchased ice cream wholesale from a local manufacturer and added our own quirky spin to a mobile ice cream party service. We grew the company organically and constantly improved as we went along. For the first year, all we did was buy ice cream and show up to parties serving ice cream and playing real music with a lounge area. That was all we needed to become profitable and to start the minimal viable product of our overall goal. Starting small makes you focus on solving real problems for people. Starting scrappy and getting super creative with limited resources gives you a stronger foundation from which to grow. It eliminates the friction of big infrastructure and gets right to the point. It will allow your company to easily pivot and enable you to keep your ear to the ground for customer feedback.

So, no, your idea doesn't need funding to start. You also don't need an MBA, a particular big client, a certain person's endorsement, a lucky break, or any other common excuse used not to start. Just get off your butt and Carpe Noodle! That's right Seize the Noodle, and unlock the creativity to start your business today!

I wrote this book to show you how to break things down so you can start! I will give you step-by-step instructions that will help you make good preliminary decisions, build a lean business that has a chance to succeed, and grow your business for success. All on a Ramen Noodle budget! I'm not going to give you more work than is absolutely necessary. I'm going to make it so easy you're going to wish you did this years ago! But before we get started, I want to make one thing clear: this book is about how to start, so you won't find accounting spreadsheets and business plan templates here. We are focusing on tackling the fear that prevents most people from starting a business and truly following their dream . . .

So if you're ready to build your own dream on a Ramen Noodle budget, keep on reading!

Working 8 hours a day in a job that you hate can undoubtedly hurt the quality of your life and cause a range of emotional, mental, and physical problems—not to mention its effect on your personal relationships as well.

Have you ever sat at work wondering, "What if I just let go?" "What if I could start my own business and be my own boss?"—hoping that you could live a more fulfilling and rewarding life? Then welcome to the club! Most people are absolutely desperate to go through with it and turn their lives around; however, very few of them actually know HOW TO DO IT. They're not prepared, and they're too frightened to take the leap into unknown territory, worried that everything will come crashing down around them because they don't have what it takes (the money or the skills) to start a business.

With my guidance and your effort, you, too, can build an awesome business! And you don't need hundreds and thousands of dollars to do it either! All you need is to think it through, set up a simple plan that you can follow, and listen to someone (me!) who will tell you what you really need to do.

Every "Start a Business" textbook will take you through a very dry course on how to write a business plan, research for weeks or months, hire experts to do this or that, and how to research the legal issues you'll have to deal with. A few chapters in, you realize that you need at least $100,000 to follow through with every step mentioned. Do you really want to read 300 pages of instructions that make your dreams seem further and harder to reach? Personally, I'd rather have a crash course that takes me through the basics, and skip all the fluff and BS that I don't really need. I want to read something that leaves me feeling confident and more knowledgeable about the steps I need to take to start my business. Reading 300 pages of dry content isn't going to help anyone but the optician when you need a new pair of eye glasses!

> Done is better than perfect

This book, on the other hand, is a crash course in the kick-butt principles of starting a business, designed specifically for entrepreneurs-in-the-making who have a unique business idea and are ready to bring it to life. Most of the information here comes from my own personal experience—because I believe that the best advice comes from someone who has been there and done that. That's why I have included personal stories and anecdotes, because there's nothing quite like hearing it from someone who was standing in your shoes at one time, someone who managed to break into the business and become successful from an idea. At one point, I was where you are now. I had dreams and hopes and ambitions, but I was also held back by fear of the unknown and a million questions that I didn't have the answers to. I hope you will be able to learn from my experiences and discover that you can survive even the most difficult times and come through successfully.

With all that, some people still need permission to follow their dreams and others need a hard push and maybe even a kick! So here it is!

TEST YOUR IDEA

What's your business idea?

How can you test it in 24 hours?

A week?
_____

A month?
_____

Describe your idea in 140 characters or less.
_____

Who in your network will champion your idea?
_____

Who are your haters?
_____

Now delete your haters from your phone, email, and life!

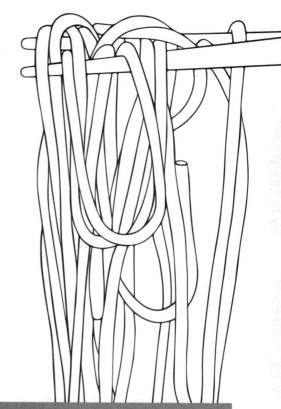

Chapter 2

Carpe Noodle!

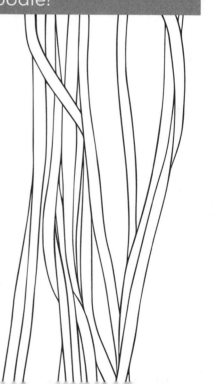

Chapter 2
Carpe Noodle!

> "I'd rather have a life of 'Oh Wells' than a life of 'What Ifs'."

> ~Kathryn Finey—Digitalundivided

We've all been super strapped for cash at some point in our lives, times when you hardly had enough money to feed your growling stomach. For most of us that time was college or maybe, for you, it's this very minute.

And now, you may find yourself in a situation where you have a brilliant business idea that you are just sitting on, day after day and month after month, because everyone says you need to have millions in startup capital, go through rounds of Venture Capital funding, or take out massive loans that you have no clue how or if you will ever be able to pay back. The world looks bleak, everything seems to be working against you, and just thinking about all the hoops you have to jump through gives you heartburn.

Let's throw all of those obstacles out the window for a moment and think positively instead. Do you remember how you were able to accomplish the impossible back in college without your parents' money? You shared a house with 4 to 10 other people and had to fend for yourself. Back when a cup of Ramen Noodles was your ultimate best friend, you'd find creative ways to turn it into a gourmet meal, adding your own special seasoning, pieces of delicious chicken or shrimp, and, if you were feeling really fancy, you'd add a few candles to the dinner table!

How were you able to get so creative with such a limited starting point of a package of Ramen Noodles? In the next few chapters we're going to bring that scrappy Ramen Noodle creativity back! That same creativity that lead you to turn Ramen Noodles into a gourmet meal to feed your friends and family is what we are going to harness to help you start and grow a successful business. I'm going to shake you up and turn you into an entrepreneur who's driven for success. Now is the time to harness that **Ramen Noodle Creativity!**

For most people, turning a hobby into a business is a far-off dream. That's mostly due, in part, to the fact that we've all encountered dream-crushers ever since we were kids—whether it was our classmate telling us we couldn't open a mud pie restaurant in the middle of the playground or our parents telling us to pursue med school instead of art because they wanted us to have secure and successful lives. (*Sometimes our parents are our biggest dream-crushers.*)

The reason you struggle so much is that you are literally battling yourself in order to follow your dreams. Our traditional education system equips students with the tools needed to enter the workforce, but it does not help students catapult their unique ideas. Therefore, in order to follow your dreams, you have to erase much of what you learned and relearn a new way of believing in yourself and your ideas to put something amazing out into the world.

Starting a business can seem pretty overwhelming with so many imagined and real obstacles in your way, preventing you from reaching your dreams. You may be thinking . . .

- I don't have enough money. I have no business training.
- I don't have any support or resources.
- No one would really want to buy my stuff or use my services anyways.
- I don't have enough money.
- And, I don't even know where to start!

However, the truth is a different matter entirely. Everyone can turn their passion into a lucrative business! If you are creative enough, your startup costs could equal just a few packs of Ramen Noodles. The only catch is: it doesn't happen overnight. And honestly, since when did dreams ever become reality overnight? We create our own reality, and if our reality is based on what we are passionate about, we are happier, more well-adjusted people. I am not going to paint you a rosy picture—building a business takes a lot of sweat, time, and energy. But it's all worth it!

Not following your dreams will not only cost you sweat, time and energy, it will also eat away at you each day because you are not living your full potential. Negative thoughts like those listed above are your greatest obstacles (think of negativity as your archenemy on this journey). They can and will prevent you from leading the life you deserve, running a business you love, and forever freeing you from the dreaded cubicle nation.

No Training

Most small businesses are started by people with no business training at all. Trust me, I was one of them. We built a successful gourmet popsicle business with no formal culinary experience. In fact, the only food experience I had was working at McDonald's at age 16 and cooking up Ramen Noodles and hot dogs in high school and college.

No Money

Many do not have a pile of cash stowed away for start-up costs—again that was me! We initially started the business spending $1200 of our savings to purchase two tricycle ice cream carts online.

Here is a very important nugget of business wisdom that I am going to impart to you. If you create a product that is in demand . . . someone will buy your product. If you offer a service that people need . . . someone will hire you. It's that simple.

Don't Know Where to Start

As for not knowing where to start? This is one of the most common problems people claim to have when starting a new business. You start where you are, with what you have. The key to starting a business on a Ramen Noodle budget is getting creative and being committed to slow and sustainable growth. I, as the founder and Chief Popsicle of Feverish Pops, along with my husband Derick Pearson, pioneered the gourmet popsicle trend, and we started a globally recognized and sought-after brand with a Fortune 500 client list that included Google, Forever 21, Paypal, Airbnb, and Whole Foods Market, in my parents' backyard, with no experience, no connections, and very, very little money. What I did have was a scrappy creative mindset, and, I would have to say, I learned my first lessons in marketing and scrappy creativity in high school.

If you could major in anything in high school, I majored in the two Bs. It was a double major—boys and basketball. That's right! Hey, I was a 15-year-old girl; we have our priorities. I spent all my time on the telephone or playing basketball and not on my homework, books, or paying attention to teachers.

I was forced to learn how to get super creative with limited resources because I was determined to go to college. In my senior year of high school, my guidance counselor told me that I would never make it to college with my then 2.7 GPA. I ended up using her words as motivation, and I won over $120,000 in scholarships. I got creative, filling out a gazillion applications, and learning very early on how to make scholarship judges focus on the things that I excelled in, like community service or writing—and not my lackluster grades.

During my 3.5 years at Lynn University, I majored in Communications, and when I left, I worked for some really cool companies. My last full-time "cubicle" job was working for the NBA as the Front Office Marketing Manager for its Minnesota WNBA team. Among other things, I was responsible for the 10th Anniversary rebranding campaign. I quit that job with dreams of opening up a hipster ice cream truck back home in Florida. But I put those dreams aside to travel the country working for Nintendo.

My short-lived dream job was working as an Experiential Marketing Tour Manager with Nintendo's experiential marketing firm USMP. My job was to travel around the country, putting together big, larger-than-life experiential events, so that consumers could experience the games before they could buy them. To put it lightly, I ABSOLUTELY loved my job.

Sometimes, a great and well-paying job will stand in the way of living our full potential, just as a dead-end job can. It's counter-intuitive: the stability of a job that doesn't feel like a dead-end job because of the pay or high-growth potential might actually stop us from truly following what excites us.

The most popular question I get from people I meet is "How did you start Feverish?" My answer is simple: I fell into the business. Actually, it was more like a trip, stumble, and epic fall.

Two years before starting Feverish, I was leaving a party and, like clockwork, as soon as I walked out of the gate, an ice cream truck drove by. I heard the music, and I turned into a 5-year-old kid again and started chasing after it. I completely forgot that I was wearing heels. I am sure you can guess what happened next. Yep, I fell flat on my face, chasing after an ice cream truck in heels!

I looked left and right to make sure no one was laughing at me, and I saw the ice cream truck driver. Thankfully, he stopped, but he was laughing at me.

Two big ideas came to me while I was on the pavement:

1. *I'm way too old to be chasing after an ice cream truck.*

And,

2. *Why hasn't anyone come up with a cooler way for adults to enjoy ice cream?*

That was my, Oprah "Ah-hah!" moment. I toyed with the second question for about two years. I had a sketchbook with different ideas, drawings, pictures, and inspiration from the internet, like the old-school Pinterest (*Darn, I should have invented Pinterest.*) But I really loved what I was doing in experiential marketing at the time, so I let it go.

While I was working with Nintendo, my husband and I both worked on the team that launched the Wii Fit and Wii Sports Resort campaigns. Unfortunately, the economy started going downhill in 2008, our contracts ended, and we both ended up unemployed.

So I thought . . . "Now is the time to move back to Florida and start this thing." When I say we started on a super-low budget, it's an understatement. I started by purchasing two ice cream carts from the luxury shopping website Craigslist. (It's like Bloomingdale's for broke people.) I had no money for a fancy graphic wrap, so I spray-painted and decorated them completely by myself with whatever I could find at Home Depot.

We put up a free profile on MyPartyPlanner.com and Myspace.com. I literally started showing up at high-end events with the hope that someday someone would actually pay me to be there. (*That's called Positioning. Not asking for permission, but doing what needs to be done and asking for forgiveness later. We positioned ourselves in the rooms that we wanted to be invited to and the events that we wanted to be paid to cater. We didn't have the contacts, but we had our product and knew that we could either stay at home hoping and wishing or we could put ourselves in situations that would give us the best likelihood of bumping into decision makers. And, most importantly, because they saw us at high-end events, they would now see our budding brand as high-end also ...Winning!)*

For a while, I was just trying to figure out what the heck I was doing and how I was going to make money off of this wacky idea. Sometimes I gave away free ice cream because I was afraid to sell it, but after a while, I built up the confidence to show up at places and sell. I figured out a few things really early.

I knew that I didn't want to drive around neighborhoods and sell to kids, because that market was saturated. Also, the last thing I wanted was people I knew laughing at me and saying, "Oh my gosh, look at what happened to Felecia's life after college. I thought she was such a promising student." I knew I wanted to create something that was really different and that was tailored towards adults. That's when we decided to focus on offering unique ice cream and specializing in ice cream catering, with just a little bit of street vending.

We ran carts and kiosks. Inside our store, we made gourmet popsicles with really unique flavors, like Pineapple Basil, Raspberry and Sweet Tea Vodka, Chocolate Salted Coconut, Mango Bourbon, Peanut Butter & Jelly, and Strawberry Balsamic. Everything is vegan-friendly, and we have a line of spiked popsicles made with all-natural, organic ingredients and organic evaporated cane juice as a sweetener. We produced everything locally in our Midtown Miami shop. And our client roster grew to include big clients—Google, Airbnb, Paypal, Cadillac, JCrew, Jameson Whiskey, William Sonoma, Adidas, Forever 21, Cirque du Soleil, Tom Cruise, Whole Foods, BB&T Bank, Universal Music, Capital Records, Vitamin Water, The Ritz-Carlton, Reebok, Trump Hotel, and the U.S. Census Bureau, just to name a few. I could go on and on naming all of the cool clients that we've been able to work with.

Our claim to fame was our line of spiked popsicles that we launched in 2011.

> What kills us most is this BS idea of what success means that is rooted in what society tells us success is supposed to look like.
>
> You want to know how to be successful?
>
> Individualize it.
>
> Determine what success and failure mean to you.
>
> You—and only you!

A cocktail on a stick! Offering such a unique concept and product has garnered lots of media attention from outlets such as *The Today Show*, the Cooking Channel, *Forbes Travel*, Inc.com, Entrepreneur.com, Grio100, *Essence* magazine, the *Boston Globe*, *Wall Street Journal Japan*, UrbanDaddy, Daily Candy, the *Miami Herald*, AllBusiness.com, and *The Wall Street Journal's* Market Watch.

We were honored at the Empact 100 Awards at the White House for being one of the Top 100 Entrepreneurs under the age of 30 in 2011. Other honors included Top 10 Superstar Entrepreneurs by AllBusiness.com, Best Ice Pops in the US by MSN, TheGrio's 100—Top 100 African Americans Making History, and White House Champions of Change for STEM access in 2014 for our work with Code Fever. Mother Nature Networks named us one of the Top 10 Eco-Friendly food businesses in 2010.

All of the great media attention and accolades helped us launch our PopPreneurs Entrepreneurship Training Program, which taught young kids how to launch their own pop business, and now Code Fever, an in-school and weekend program that engages minority teens in technology development and entrepreneurship, after Feverish was acquired in 2015. I now spend the majority of my time spearheading Code Fever and advising startups.

Together, my husband Derick, our business partner Joe, and I packaged and created this really exciting brand, powered by social media, crazy guerrilla marketing, and a great customer experience starting on a Ramen Noodle Budget and exploding into a globally recognized brand. That's how we catapulted our brand from scratch, with just a little over a thousand dollars back in 2008.

And that's what I'm going to show you how to do in this book. Are you ready?

What does success mean to you?

What does failure mean to you?

WHAT SCREWS US UP MOST IN LIFE IS THE PICTURE IN OUR HEAD OF HOW IT IS SUPPOSED TO BE.

Six very compelling reasons to
FIRE YOUR BOSS!

1 **A recession is a terrible thing to waste:**
You've heard that a brain is a terrible thing to waste? Well, I think a recession is a terrible thing to waste, and as America continues its slow marathon towards recovery, it provides amazing opportunities for Ramen Noodle Startups—if you know where to look. Prices are cheaper, materials are cheaper, vendors are more willing to negotiate, and fellow entrepreneurs are more willing to barter. Another thing to consider is that there is less competition. Unfortunately, many businesses closed down in the downturn, leaving a lot of sectors wide open for a creative Ramen Noodle entrepreneur like you!

2 **Cutbacks and no raises:**
If you are working for someone else, you are building their dream and not your own. You no longer have to watch the owner of the company drive away in a new BMW while you putt-putt around in a ten-year-old station wagon. The BMW was the business owner's dream, but the work you did in creating the profits for his company paid for it! We all want to see the work we do finally benefit ourselves instead of someone else. After all, you want to buy your own BMW, right? Or maybe a fuel-efficient Prius?

3 **Growing lack of job security:**
Budget cuts and the ailing economy are causing downsizing and layoffs. Gone are the days of working for a company for 40+ years. There is no loyalty on either end these days. It's not easy to go out and get another job. Many people have been laid off or are college grads who cannot find a job in their field. The competition is tough, and there is a lot of it. When you are the business owner, no one can fire you. Your position is secure for as long as you want it, or for as long as your business makes a profit. You know what really sucks? Spending $50,000+ on a college education and having to settle for being a waitress because you're afraid to start your dream business.

4 Reduction in benefits:

Many employees are not being offered the benefits that were available just ten or twenty years ago—or heck, even five years ago. In addition, the unstable stock market is causing employees to lose money from their retirement accounts. As an entrepreneur, you can guarantee any number of benefits for yourself and be in a position to decide how you want to invest and manage your retirement funds.

5 Family needs:

The need to take care of our family members is increasing. Some families can't afford care for their elders, and some can't afford childcare. It's not uncommon for a family to spend more on daycare expenses than they earned for a given time period. Owning a business gives you the flexibility to care for your loved ones and have more of your own money available for expenses. Think of it not just from a financial standpoint; think about not being able to control your own time. When I worked at an advertising agency, I worked 12-hour days; they owned my time and practically my life. I dreaded the thought of having kids and not being able to see them except on Saturdays and Sundays.

6 Freedom and control over your life:

We've all seen those commercials on TV, the ones that portray people telling us that they made $10,000 in one week while only working part time. They have wonderful houses, new cars, and every conceivable luxury known to mankind. Does it always work like this? No. But do you have the potential to direct your own schedule and control your time? Definitely. The more successful your business is, the more control you will have over your time.

So you've done it . . . you are powered up . . . you read the 6 reasons to fire your boss, and you just gave him or her the pink slip! You've made that final decision to start your own business. But where will it go? Where do you want it to go? Setting goals is important for any successful business. Your business will tempt you into excelling in order to stay at the top and outshine your competitors. You won't fall into an unhealthy routine when you have a clear plan of what needs to be done. You'll find new challenges and set new heights for yourself to achieve. The most successful businesses are those that are strategically moving forward.

Keep that in mind and never stop moving forward.

Now, without further ado, let's get down to how you can start a business on a Ramen Noodle budget!

To your success,

Felecia Hatcher & Derick Pearson
–former Chief Popsicles
Feverish Pops

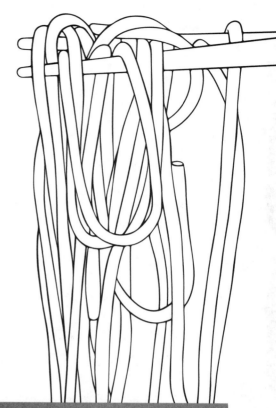

Chapter 3

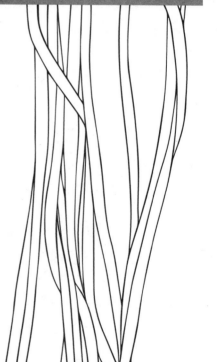

Starting on a Ramen Noodle Budget

Chapter 3
Starting on a Ramen Noodle Budget

> "Doesn't matter if the glass is half-empty or half-full. All that matters is that you are the one pouring the glass."

~Mark Cuban

Starting a business on a Ramen Noodle budget is code for "starting a business while you're broke." You have to figure out what your passion is first and then how to turn your passion into a profit. Following your passion is the best way to start a successful and sustainable business, grow it organically, create a loyal following, and, best of all, create an all-around, kick-butt brand.

Following your passion helps you stay true to your brand, service other people, and do it the way you want to do it. Its sounds very cliché, but if you don't follow your passion and just do it for the money, over time, customers are going to be able to tell that it's not authentically you, and they're not going to support it. Or eventually you're going to grow to hate it and grow to hate yourself.

The best thing about starting a business is that essentially, you get to inject your personality, your talents, and your skills into a product or service that solves a problem. But you have to figure out who you are, what you love to do, and what you don't love to do in order to start a business that is going to kick-butt and take names.

Go back a little bit and try to remember those days when you were in school. Every now and then, I'm asked to speak at elementary school assemblies, and when I talk to those kids, they are so excited. They want to do some of the coolest things with their lives. Somewhere down that line, usually around fifth or sixth grade, it changes.

When you're 4 or 5 years old, if you think you can fly, what are you going to do? You tie a towel around your neck, climb to the highest point in your parents' living room, and jump! Pretending to be your favorite superhero. You're not going to ask anyone's permission. You don't grab your box of crayons to fill out a business plan—absolutely not.

You jump from the highest point. If you fall and hurt yourself, you don't care. You get right back up and find the next highest point and jump again. You continue to jump and jump and jump until you either get tired or until your parents say, "Knock it off!" And then you still do it!

The point is, in that moment, you totally believe in yourself and all inhibitions are set aside. Whatever anybody thinks of you doesn't matter—you just do what you want to do. There's beauty in that. But as we get older, we start to let other people influence us and tell us what our passion is or what we are good at. Only you truly know what you are the best at. It's about following your passion and figuring out the best way to monetize it.

> Stop sitting on your genius!
> Start today with what you have and where you are!

I often like to tell the story about a guy who started a company called Big Man Bakes. The founder, Chip Brown, was in med school, and every night when he was doing his rounds for his residency, he would always bring cupcakes for all of his co-workers. They absolutely loved it and started to place orders.

Mind you, this guy is not your average baker! He looks like he played football in college or the NFL. With a 6´5″ line-backer build, he spent every waking minute baking. He finally dropped out of medical school and started his own cupcake shop called Big Man Bakes in Downtown Los Angeles. He was featured on the *Oprah* show, which you and I both know is the golden endorsement!

Big Man Bakes is a true testament to following your passion.

However, it cost him a few hundred thousand dollars in student loans from medical school before he found it, instead of following his passion first. But, in time, he figured out how to make money off of his passion.

That's what you have to do, too. For me, finding my passion was not so much about knowing what I wanted to do, but knowing what I *did not* want to do. I worked for the NBA when I was around 23 as a front office Marketing Manager for the Minnesota Timberwolves. I may have been the youngest person in the league to have that job. I was the head of the marketing department for the WNBA franchise. It was a great job . . . for someone who was passionate about it.

I played basketball in high school, and I love technology and marketing, but I didn't love that job. I really struggled to wake up every single day, and I finally had to start paying attention to it. I was saying to myself, "Why do I hate my existence at 7 a.m. every morning when I have to wake up? Why am I here in this −30° weather in Minnesota? I hate being in an office every single day and only interacting with the 3 people I share a cubicle with. As a matter of fact, I hate being in a cubicle."

A lot of things were eating away at my soul, and I finally had to say, "You know what, Felecia? This is not what you want to do. What you want to do is open up an ice cream truck." I would tell my co-workers that all the time, and they would laugh at me.

But a funny thing happened . . .

After we were featured on the Cooking Channel, one of my former co-workers e-mailed me to say, "Oh my God, you really did it!" For me, that was probably one of the brightest moments of my life, because I had talked about this religiously for the eight months that I worked there. And I finally did what I said I was going to do.

I love what I do every single day because it is the biggest creative outlet for me. I am a creative person who loves working with my hands. I have an office and a desk now, and I barely sit at it. I love the creative freedom to work wherever I want to work and interact with people all day long about things I love. This is what I'm great at, and it brings me the most joy. I figured out the way to creatively tap into my passion and turn it into a profit in the form of desserts on a stick.

So, what's your passion? Dig deep into your soul and find it.

NOW.

Wow, that word is so short, but it means so much. So, let's get this straight—postponing everything until later isn't going to cut it . . . and it isn't what this book is all about either. You want something, you go for it **NOW**. You shouldn't read the rest of this book without having at least a vague idea of what you want to do. So, I would like you to take a few moments and complete the short exercise below, so that you and I both know what it is you're hoping to accomplish—what business are you so passionate about that you would want to spend the rest of your life doing it? (Some people will even want to work through retirement when they do something they love so much.) This is a time to be radically honest with yourself. I find that deep down everyone knows what they want to do but are afraid to admit it to themselves.

Grab a pen and sit somewhere quiet where you can't be disturbed.

Now list three to five hobbies, things you're great at, or things you're very passionate about.

What am I passionate about?	How can I make money?	Can I turn this into a successful business?

Next, for each of those you listed, answer these questions:

- "How can I make money out of this?"
- "Can I turn this into a successful business?"

Make sure you write down EVERYTHING that goes through your mind, every idea and concern. Don't for a minute think that you have an idea you'll never forget and rely on memory. I want it all down on paper now!

Now that you have them all down, go through your list and try to cross some off. If you have one thing you are positive is for you, then all the better.

And that's that. You've just picked a business that revolves around YOUR passions, YOUR happiness, YOUR talents—and not the other way around. There's nothing worse than having to put the fire out from under our dreams and passions because we have to learn a certain skill-set and routinely perform a 9-to-5 job we may be good at, but we don't love. People who do that will wake up one day and realize that they've literally blown their lives away, hardly remembering when they started working for a certain company and how they stayed there for so long when they didn't get anything out of it creatively.

I can't imagine anything worse than going back to my "safe" job now!

If you have decided that you can be more successful in your own business than you would be working for someone else, then there is just one more step to complete before you take the plunge.

Make sure owning a business is what you really want!

The only person who can tell you if you are ready to start your own business is you. It's much easier to get another job than it is to start a business. Would you rather have the security of a steady paycheck? Or, would you rather go it alone, make sacrifices, and hang in there with your business until it becomes profitable? You are the only one who can answer these questions. If the idea of getting another job terrifies you, being a business owner may be an option. Remember, however, that owning a business is still a career; it's a career that you give yourself and that you can actually pass on to your kids and family once you are gone.

"WHETHER YOU THINK
YOU CAN,
OR YOU THINK
YOU CAN'T
–YOU'RE RIGHT."

Henry Ford

Getting Rid of Head Junk

Alright, Ramen Noodle Entrepreneurs, let's talk about all the junk that is constantly going around in your head and all that outside stuff that people have told you about starting a business. If you want to start a business on a Ramen Noodle budget, you have to throw out conventional thinking. **Now!**

I started my first business at the age of 19 as a college freshman. After winning all those scholarship dollars, of course my mom's friends and family asked me, "How did you do it? Can you show my kid how to do it? Can you show me how to do it? Show me the money!" I started spending all this time doing it for free.

I absolutely loved helping others, but it was getting a little tedious, and my mom said, "You need to start charging people. You can seriously turn this into a business."

I responded, "Whatever, mom."

But she was adamant in saying, "You need to charge people for it and turn it into a business."

I had no idea how to go about it. I was a top Girl Scout cookie seller when I was in elementary school; however, I had no idea what it meant to start a business. But I decided, "Okay I am going to step out on faith and see where this goes"

I read tons of business and marketing books. I tried to figure things out. Of course, I didn't have any money. I won $120,000 in scholarships and grants, but it went straight to Lynn University—I had to figure out a way to turn this idea into a real business.

So I pretty much turned my dorm room into an office. The company was called Urban Excellence, and it was an educational consulting business where we consulted and ran workshops for students and parents. We also built scholarship and college-prep programs for schools and organizations. Together my business partner, James Taylor, and I built the business on a super low budget. We used and abused our college campus and all of its free resources.

That's why I tell students while you are in college, while you are in high school, middle school, elementary school, coming out of the womb, this is the best time to start a business because you don't have any of the financial responsibilities and obligations that you will have once you get out of college. You don't have the mortgage, and you probably don't have any kids, car payments, student loans, etc. If you took out student loans, they're deferred for the next four years, so you don't have any major financial obligations. That is why this is the best time.

If you start a business and it fails, so what? FAIL FAST, learn from your mistakes, and move on. At least you know you've got the wits to survive, especially if you're starting it on a Ramen Noodle budget. Failure is not final unless you stop trying, building, creating, and innovating.

But we're not talking about mistakes and failures right now. We're talking about success.

Why is this the best time? The opportunities that are available to you—the resources, mentors, and the business plan competitions—you won't see that once you graduate. You may find business plan competitions, but that's nowhere near the amount that takes place on your college campus with the abundant amount of money available and the few students competing for them. Since not many college students are starting businesses, the pool of competitors for those awards is really small. This is the best time to start a business!

So much technology is available to us today that makes it easier to start a business cheaper and faster. We all look up to Richard Branson, Steve Jobs, Bill Gates, and Oprah Winfrey, but think about the advantage we have over Oprah when she was just getting started thirty years ago. Back then, Oprah had a fro, Twitter was just a sound, Facebook's founder was in diapers, Foursquare was a parking space, LinkedIn was a prison, and the Cloud was in the sky. So what's your excuse?

As young entrepreneurs, you have to take advantage of everything that is now available to you and stop with the excuses. You have no other choice. With the economy the way it is right now, jobs aren't waiting for you at all. You have to hustle and really bust your butt to get a job these days. If you do get one, you'll be lucky if it's in your field or if it pays enough that you can actually pay off your debts and move out of your parents' house.

Create Your Own Job!

The beauty of starting a business is that you are your own boss, and only you dictate how much money you make. The harder you work, the more you make. If you are working for someone else, you're working on salary. Say you get a job making $70,000 a year out of college (you'd be lucky to find that!). But you also have to consider that no matter how hard you work, you're never going to make more than that $70,000 a year until your raise comes up—if you're lucky enough to get one on an annual basis.

There was a time in corporate America when you were only supposed to work 40 hours a week, but now it's leaning towards 60. You're answering your phone on the weekends at 2:00 or 3:00 in the morning, 4:00 a.m. text messages and e-mails, and you're bringing your work home with you every single night—and you still won't make more than that $70,000.

But as an entrepreneur and a business owner, the harder you work, the more return you will get. If I need to go out and make money right now, I'll push one of our popsicle carts out, sell some popsicles, and bring money back. Honestly, sometimes it's as simple as that.

Understand that you deserve this. You deserve to own your own business. You deserve to build generational wealth for your family for years and years to come. Heck, start a business with the intent to sell it. Do what you need to do right now to start this business. Clear that slate in your head, and let's get this thing rolling

You have to throw out all the conventional thinking and everything people have told you that you need to do to start a business. The main thing you need to do right now is this . . .

throw out conventional thinking

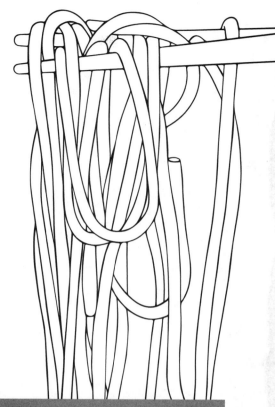

Chapter 4

Stretching the Noodle

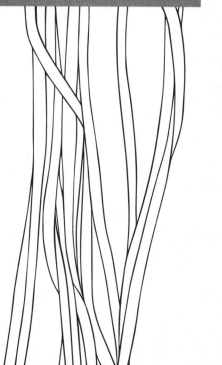

Chapter 4
Stretching the Noodle

> "One cannot be prepared
> for something while secretly
> believing it will never happen."
>
> ~Nelson Mandela

Having the right mindset to achieve anything in life is the most important part of attaining a goal. Both failure and success are the result of a certain state of mind. One of the most important steps to becoming successful in your business, financially free and wealthy, is a change in mindset.

And I'm going to stress this point: It has to happen NOW—before anything else!

The "self-fulfilling prophecy" may be a term that you've heard before. It's basically a prediction that comes true simply because whoever is predicting it believes that it will. So, by the act of making the prediction and believing, we bring the prediction to fruition. That is what having the successful mindset is all about—making a prediction for your success and believing that you will be successful thereby brings about your success. If you, of all people, do not believe that you are capable of succeeding, then your failure is quite easy to predict.

The bottom line is that you have to believe that you can achieve success and wealth before you will ever be able to reach it. The limits to which you subject yourself are the limits that will prevent it from happening. If you look for reasons rather than results, then you will have sabotaged yourself before you ever make it out of the starting gate. Believe it can happen . . . and it will!

An important part of achieving success is first understanding and determining why you want what you want. The stronger the desire and reason to achieve something, the quicker and easier it is to achieve it. You need to take a moment to think of the reasons why you want to build wealth before starting out on your journey. Your reasons provide the fuel and drive for achieving success. Without them, you're doomed to fail because there's no passion or drive to do better, achieve more, and stick with it.

A lot of people imagine that they can start a business one day and get rich the next. It doesn't work that way; every successful business takes hard work, determination, and unrealistic goals with a realistic action plan. (Yes, that's right, I said *unrealistic* goals!)

All you need to set up your list of unrealistic goals is to throw out conventional thinking and create your plan toward success!

Goals put things into perspective for you and supply you with detailed steps on how to get there. Behind every business failure is someone who chose to listen to naysayers, chose not to follow a strategic plan, chose to take shortcuts, and chose not to write down any goals.

Setting up unrealistic goals is a powerful tool to use in your professional and personal life. I like to tell people to set goals that seem so far out of reach that they have no idea if they will ever be able to come close to them because that's where the magic happens.

Have you ever heard the saying "reach for the moon, and if you fail, you may land among the stars"? I've always made goals that seemed out of reach, but then I positioned myself to make those goals happen. For example, several years ago, I made a personal goal that I wanted to be featured on *Good Morning America*. I didn't have a publicist or any media contacts, so at the time, it was a very unrealistic goal. I started to work on things to promote Feverish and position my company so that it was more attractive to the media. I expanded on Search Engine Optimization for our website, and we ended up getting featured on NBC's *Today Show* in February 2012!

The magic happens outside of our comfort zone.

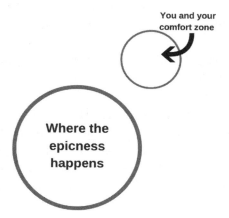

You and your comfort zone

Where the epicness happens

Creating a Goal Planning Sheet

I am a very visual person—even if I have to use a paper napkin or the back of my hand when I set goals, I write them down. Decide what type of goals you need to set. They need to be so big that they make you very uncomfortable, because that is where the magic happens. Remember, your goals can be both long-term and short-term and can include both personal and professional aims. Make separate lists for all groupings that fit into your life: Family, Work, Business, Health, Finance, and so on. This will help you find that balance in your life and reach where you want to be.

Write three tiers of goals: immediate/short-term, long-term, and unrealistic. The short-term goals are immediate—for example, if you want to create a chocolate company, go to the grocery store, pick up the necessary ingredients, and make chocolate this weekend. Get the recipe where you want it to be.

A long-term goal could be to get a booth at an upcoming event and have a batch of your chocolate ready to sell that weekend. Break the long-term goals into easier-to-manage, short-term goals that you can achieve a lot easier and in a much shorter timeframe.

Then the unrealistic goal could be this: Get featured on "Oprah's Favorite Things List" or have your chocolate sold at every Whole Foods in the nation! Why not? When I mention unrealistic goals, we're talking about dreaming BIG.

My Most Epic Dream Is? _____

(You fill in the blank.)

Even with unrealistic goals, your goals should be as detailed as possible. Elaborate and make sure you add a timeframe for the completion of the goal (e.g., within the next year). Many people wish to be billionaires and say it every day but never take the time to outline the small steps they can take every day to better position themselves to be billionaires or identify the people within their network that they can delegate or outsource to make their dreams become a reality.

Set up daily and weekly reminders on your phone. Just like you would set up a doctor's appointment reminder on your phone, do the same thing for your goals. Our cell phones are really the only thing that we all travel with 24/7. If you are anything like me, my phone goes with me to the bathroom and sleeps under my pillow. (*I know I am not the only one who texts on the toilet, so don't even go there!*)

Contemplate your goals while you work to achieve them, and always make time to celebrate your success, because you and only you will know the sacrifice and hard work it took to achieve your goals.

As your priorities change, so should your goals. What your business strives for right now could and should be very different from what it strives for a year from now.

Don't try to do everything at once, especially when working toward long-term goals. This can be too taxing and complicated. It's important to continue feeling that you are accomplishing something, so the short-term goals help with this, in addition to bringing you one step closer to reaching your long-term goals.

> The dream is free, the hustle is sold separately.

Goals + Action = Traction

The reason most people fail at goal setting is that they don't put action behind their goals—they just put a lot of action behind the thought of it. If you want to buy a new car, what's the first step? You would research cars online, assess finances to determine how much you can afford, create a savings timeline to see if you can afford a car right away, and visit your bank to apply for an auto loan. Breaking it down into steps just made the daunting task of getting a new car a little easier, right?

In 2012, the photo-sharing app Instagram was acquired by social media giant Facebook for $1 billion. At the time, Instagram had only 4 employees and 27 million users, but it had positioned itself as a formidable threat to Facebook. (The most surprising point: the company had $0 profits!) You want to know what Instagram had? It had TRACTION!!! Traction is completely different from an idea, but investors love traction.

Disrupt Your Goals

Sometimes goals have to cancel themselves out in order to catapult you into success. When Apple came out with the iPod, it completely revolutionized the digital music market. But they practically crushed the sales of the iPod when they came out with the iPod Nano and then completely crushed it again when they came out with the iPhone. Crushing one aspect of Apple's business led the way to not only selling music but also selling apps and creating and leading in a whole new digital space.

On the flip side, let's look at Kodak, which was once a leader in the film and photography products industry. That company did not want to disrupt its film sales when consumers started leaning towards digital. It went from being the top photography company to bankruptcy because it didn't want to disrupt its business model by switching to digital as the world rapidly changed.

Don't despair when you fail at a certain goal—take the time to reflect on it instead, learn the lesson, improve, and move on. The key is to Fail Fast and Move On!

Disrupt Your Goals in 4 Easy Steps
1. Set goals so big that they scare your pants off!
2. Work backwards from your goals, and align all the people and resources that you need to make it happen.
3. Break it down into weekly actionable steps.
4. Constantly innovate and create new versions of your product or service that add value to your customers and outperform the old concept.

FAIL FAST, SUCCEED FASTER

List how you can test out your business idea and fail fast. Failing fast means getting your feet wet, putting your whole self in, and being vulnerable with your idea.

_____

_____

_____

_____

_____

_____

_____

_____

_____

_____

_____

_____

_____

_____

WHAT SCREWS US UP MOST IN LIFE IS THE **PICTURE** IN OUR HEAD OF HOW IT IS **SUPPOSED** TO BE.

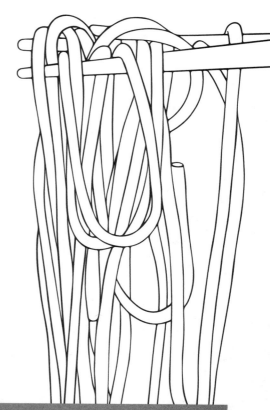

Chapter 5

Beware of the Drunken Noodle!

Chapter 5
Beware of the Drunken Noodle!

> "Business isn't a science. It's not like mixing this chemical with that chemical to get a predictable outcome. You can make a plan and set a goal and even be reasonably sure that you'll reach that goal, but until you do, you won't know if you will."

~Fred DeLuca, Founder and CEO of Subway

Beware of the Drunken Noodle!
What? That's right, I said it. When you're doing your research on starting a business or even just speaking with people, they'll tell you, "Oh, you need to incorporate right away, hire employees, blah, blah, blah." Or, you might be observing other entrepreneurs, looking at where they are and comparing it to where you currently are. It can all be a little daunting. Often, when we're doing too much research and not enough experimenting, we can educate ourselves out of our dreams. It's unfortunate, but it happens.

I don't want that happening to you, though. I remember when I started Urban Excellence, my first business, I would pick up every single book looking for the exact step-by-step roadmap on how to start a business and grow it. I thought I would find a step-by-step blueprint or road map with GPS and turn-by-turn directions, I kid you not!

My mentor at the time finally said to me, "Felecia, put down the damn books." He said, "You're never going to find the answers that you're looking for in a book because no one has ever done what you're doing before. Even if they have, the environment is no longer the same. You're not going to find a blueprint."

No one is ever going to provide you with step-by-step instructions on what to do. Even when you buy a franchise, the environment in which the original business was created can never be duplicated. You have to think about it this way: when Oprah or Richard Branson started to build their businesses thirty years ago, the internet as we know it now didn't even exist yet! So the exact steps that they took can never be duplicated because the world is completely different now.

You have to put down the books (except this one, of course), and be confident in the steps that you're going to take. A lot of what makes a successful entrepreneur is just stepping out on blind faith. As they say, leap and the net will appear. Make a decision to catapult your life, and make changes as you go. As mistakes happen, embrace them, and just keep moving forward! Eventually, you'll find your way. You'll find your stride, but you're not going to find a step-by-step guide in a book.

Even though I caution you to not educate yourself away from your dream, I'm not saying you shouldn't do any research. You definitely want to understand the industry that you're getting yourself into. But in order to start a business on a Ramen Noodle budget, there's some BS you've heard that you're going to need to throw out in order to start, grow it organically, and build a successful and sustainable business.

First Up . . . Incorporating

This is the "I need to Look Official before I'm Official" syndrome.

I know business professors and some business professionals may not agree with me (and I am sure Uncle Sam does not agree with me). So many people get obsessed with this aspect of the business for the sake of feeling official that they neglect the important part. It's better if you've sold your first product or gotten your first client before you legally start the business. You also need to delay some of the big costs when you first launch your idea. That is unless it is absolutely necessary for your industry. But most of the time it is not.

Incorporating your business on the low end usually costs around $150 or so (give or take, depending on the state). On the high end, it can cost thousands to get a lawyer to do it for you. The big advantages that you will get from an LLC or INC do not happen until you are actually profitable. You can incorporate at any time if you are lucky enough for your business to take off. When you incorporate, this means you have to start paying TAXES. Before you incorporate, do your due diligence to be sure that it's actually going to make you money and that this is an idea you are going to commit to. If you decide it's not going to work or it's going to take you longer to start the business, but you already incorporated, then you still have to file an annual report every year, and you haven't made a dime. You don't want to be in this position.

If you don't file the annual report because you decided to defer what you were doing, you'll have a $500 fine to pay. You don't want the IRS to come knocking on your door. That's the main reason to delay it, because not paying taxes can break you. It can ruin your company. It can ruin you.

Hiring Employees

Many people think, "Oh, I've got to hire this person and that person," simply because they wrote a business plan that says to put an executive team together. But you won't be able to afford that on a Ramen Noodle budget. Business plans may give you the expectation that you have to hire people right away, but that is not the case. In the beginning, you're going to have to do a lot of the work yourself. It is what it is. You're trying to build a business, so you'll want to know and understand all the facets of how your business works.

When you hire vendors to start taking tasks off your plate, or you hire your first employee, you'll know how long it takes to do certain things. You will have already put an invoice together, designed a menu, designed a flyer, created your product, or any other various tasks required to make your business run. You know how long these things take to accomplish, so you'll know if they're trying to cheat you out of money or not.

You know what the big boys do? The big boys outsource outside the country. They outsource like crazy, and they pay a fraction of the costs of hiring someone locally for tasks that can be completed on a computer.

"the reason we
struggle with insecurity
is because we compare our
BEHIND-THE-SCENES
with everyone else's
HIGHLIGHT REEL."

~STEVEN FURTICK

There are some really cool websites (Elance.com, Guru.com, 99designs.com, and oDesk.com) that can connect you to some amazing talented individuals, and you might be able to hire them at a very low rate to help you run your business.

Let the Force Outsource Be With You

You don't have to be in the same space, in the same state, or even in the same country to get some amazing work done. I've hired an assistant in Wyoming and in India; contractors in India, Australia, and Taiwan; a Social Media assistant in Australia; and graphic designers in California, the Philippines, and New York. We get on conference calls, Skype, and e-mail, and we get the work done.

My assistant in India worked for me for about a year and did amazing work. I would send him something by 5 p.m., and by 6 a.m. the next morning, it was in my inbox. It was the best thing ever. I was getting work done and making money while I was sleeping. More important, I was paying $3–$9 an hour for a virtual assistant (VA), and it freed me up to work on higher-level tasks, like bringing in more clients.

Check out Elance.com or college campuses for freelancers who can design your professional website for a very low cost or possibly even free.

Free Is the New Paid

One of the greatest things about starting a business while you're in college or as a young adult is that you have a giant pool of eager talent, people who are looking to collaborate and get things done. Utilize that to build your business. High school and college students need the experience to pad their resumes, so it creates a win-win situation for the both of you.

Barter, Baby, Barter

If you're starting a marketing company, and you know somebody who's starting an accounting company, great news! That accountant is going to need marketing services, and you, as a marketing person, are going to need accounting services. Help each other out. No money has to be exchanged, and you'll get it done. That's how we do it. And that's how you do it on a Ramen Noodle budget, my friend.

Office Space

Stay away, far away from renting office space unless it is absolutely necessary. Run your business out of your dorm room or home for as long as possible. We ran Urban Excellence out of my dorm room. If you called my dorm room phone number, the answering machine said "Urban Excellence," and so did I when I answered the phone. Both my roommate and I had cell phones, and we never used that dorm phone, so I turned it into my office phone . . . "Thank you for calling Urban Excellence."

For my educational consulting company, I traveled around the country putting together college-prep programs and running workshops. If I needed to meet a client, what better place to meet than on a college campus? The library at our school was a state-of-the-art, however-many-million-dollar library, and it had conference rooms that were private. It was great! Or I met clients at Starbucks. Who cares? It was still a professional setting. Most people understand this trend, and that's how they often do business as well.

I would run my business out of my home in a heartbeat if I could, but I can't because I own a food business, and I don't want the health department coming after me. As a college student, you can use the resources that are on your campus. Most schools have culinary programs, and you can use their kitchens after hours. All churches and day-care centers have approved commercial kitchens that they barely use. You could offer to sponsor one or two events a month in exchange for paying rent.

> Do one thing every day that scares the heck out of you!

Here's a cool idea. If you need to meet with somebody, find the coolest hotel in your city, and meet them in the lobby. That is the best place to hold meetings. It's nice, it's super upscale, and it's swanky. They don't know whether you're staying there or not. The hotel staff is never going to bother you unless you decide to fall asleep. Hold your meetings there and leave. Whole Foods Market is another hidden gem during rush hour times.

When I was interviewing for marketing jobs, I would fly into cities all the time for meetings in hotel lobbies. Several times, I found out that the person who was interviewing me wasn't even staying there. He or she just held the meetings there. It's all about perception, baby!

Buying Expensive Equipment

Stay far, far away from buying new equipment unless you absolutely have to. With Feverish, we looked for used equipment or went to business liquidation auctions where a business was selling all of its assets. That's where we bought our equipment.

We made away like bandits when a local Baskin-Robbins closed and held an auction to liquidate its assets. It's important to know the off-seasons for your business, too. That's when you can score big on sites like eBay and Craigslist—you can rack up on all the equipment you need. I told you that we bought our very first carts for Feverish off the website Craigslist, remember?

So, basically, don't buy new equipment unless it's absolutely essential. You can save a ton of money by buying used equipment; just make sure, of course, that it is in good shape.

We've talked about throwing out conventional thinking and delaying the normal BS people advise you to do in order to start a business. Now let's talk about...

The 9 Things You HAVE to Do NOW to Start Your Business Today

With all the technology that is available to us today, you can start a business and build a business presence quite easily and with a much lower financial barrier to entry.

Pay close attention to the tips below:

1 **Build a prototype and pitch customers from day one.**
I recently spoke with a group of kids who are part of an entrepreneurship program. I was on the panel, and one of the girls said, "I have this candy company. Can you give me some advice on how to market it?"

I said, "Sure. Tell me about the candy."

"Well, it's chocolate that's going to look like sushi." "Okay. That sounds cool. What does it taste like?"

"I don't know what it tastes like."

"Um okay . . . what do your customers think it tastes like? What are your customers saying about it?"

"Oh, I don't know."

"What do you mean you don't know what it tastes like and your customers don't know what it tastes like?"

"Well, I've worked on this business plan for a year—me and my classmates—but we've never actually made the chocolate."

Hold up, wait a minute, time out!

The worst thing that you can do is spend a ton of money and time working on a business plan and you've never even actually touched the tangible product or tried out the service. It is the biggest mistake ever. You invest time and energy into this project, and then when you finally come to the day where you make the product, you find out it tastes like crap, or it looks like crap, or the process to make it is horrendous and time consuming, or you hate it, and you've wasted six months on a business plan.

You have to, from day one, actually create the product or actually provide the service. Do it at a super-low budget in your kitchen or living room. It doesn't matter. Create the product and test it out yourself. Go through the processes before you even start working on the business plan. It makes absolutely no sense not to test it out. Get your family members and your friends to test it out. Find out how much they would pay for it. Hell, charge them for it—make sure that it's something that is actually going to make you money!

One of the best books that I can recommend to you is a book called *The Toilet Paper Entrepreneur*. Inside the book, the author actually talks about three sheets (hence, toilet paper) and what you're going to do with them. He talks about building a prosperity plan and creating a tracking sheet and a quarterly analysis. Those are the three main things that you need for your business.

I would recommend a prosperity plan over writing a business plan any day, especially within the first year while you're still trying to figure everything out.

2 **Buy your domain name ASAP!**
Whatever name you're thinking of for your business or product, you need to buy the domain name ASAP. The main reason I tell you this is because domain names are like the name you're given at birth. Say, for instance, your birth name is Jacob. There are thousands of Jacobs in the real world, but on the internet things are different because of the thousands of Jacobs in this world there can only be one owner of Jacob.com. Once Jacob.com is taken, you're either going to have to shell out thousands of dollars to get that URL, or you are going to have to pick something else. The longer you wait to purchase your URL, the more likely someone else will buy it before you.

When I started my company, Feverish, I came up with the name because I wanted it to be more like a lifestyle. I didn't want it to be a traditional ice cream company or be perceived as a traditional ice cream company. I wanted it to be something unique and different, and so we called it Feverish. If you're feeling hot, we want to cool you down with ice cream—that was the main reason for the name.

But we had to settle on Feverish Ice Cream . . .

Why? Because I sat on this idea for about two years and did not buy the domain name for those two whole years. So, by the time I finally decided to buy the domain name, it was no longer available. That's why the company was named Feverish Ice Cream instead of Feverish.

The biggest products that we made and sold were now our gourmet popsicles, not the ice cream. In fact, for the past few years, Feverish has focused solely on gourmet popsicles.

Save yourself a lot of money and heartache—buy your domain name early and hold on to it. I probably own close to 100 domain names for the simple reason that anytime I come up with an idea or business name or whatever, even though I may not start it right away, I buy the domain name and hold on to it.

3

Set up a professional voicemail or VOIP. Get a Grasshopper.com phone number or a Google Voice phone number.

The worst thing you can do is have potential customers calling your cell phone number when you answer unprofessionally with a, "Who is this?" Or, say they're calling you at 7:00 in the morning to place an order, and you answer with your morning voice because you just woke up. You want to make sure when you're starting your Ramen Noodle–budget business that you have a professional front, and your business doesn't look like a bowl of Ramen Noodles! You want people to take you seriously, and you want customers to have no hesitation to pay your rates. If they're calling your cell phone, it's not professional. You can fix this for very little money. Google Voice is absolutely free, it will ring to your cell phone, and no one has to know. You could be 3,000 miles away from your home or your office.

I like Grasshopper.com because you're able to have extensions. It rings to a general voice mail, and then people can dial extensions to reach different staff members, partners, or departments. You can have it ring to your cell phone or your home or office phone. It's really cool, and it allows you to have that professional front and have your business taken seriously right from the start. GrassHopper.com starts at $25 a month.

Other amazing phone services to check out:

- RubyReceptionist.com
- Conversational

4

Design badass business cards. This is a big thing. Have you ever gone to a meeting or a networking event where you meet a potential client and write your contact information on a scrap of paper? Business cards are super inexpensive right now. You can get them at Vistaprint.com for a ridiculously low price. Moo.com is my personal favorite for getting cheap, high-quality business cards, and you can actually have a different message or picture on every card.

The most important aspect to consider when ordering business cards is that they must be fabulous or they will be forgotten, so make sure that they really stand out. Of all the things to spend money on, I would spend the bulk of my Ramen Noodle budget on business cards, because they are your first impression on potential customers.

We have really unique business cards. Our business cards are bright colors. Mine are hot pink, hot orange, and electric blue. On the back, we have really crazy and fun pictures of our customers enjoying our pops. They're bright, they're pink, they have just enough information, and they're on thicker card stock. People comment, "Oh my gosh, I love your card!" or "This character that you have on here, he's hilarious!" It's an instant conversation starter. It makes us memorable.

When you go to networking events, people have stacks of cards that they collect, so you want to make sure that you have a card that stands out from the rest of them because that's what gets the phone calls—and that's what gets the business going.

Check out this link for inspiration http://mashable.com/2011/07/23/business-card-designs/

5 Email.
Once you buy your domain name, use that as your email address. One of the biggest mistakes I see with entrepreneurs that are just starting out is an email address that says the business name @ a free email account such as hotmail, Gmail, or yahoo. It makes me wonder if it's a real business.

It doesn't cost much to get an email like info@feleciahatcher.com or whatever your business name is (with that domain name that you bought and saved, right?). It looks better aesthetically, and it shows that your business is professional, whether you're running it in your pajamas in your dorm room or not!

6 Social media presence.

This should actually be number one. I can honestly say that if Facebook and Twitter didn't exist, Feverish would not exist. Our strategic use of social media has been huge for connecting with customers in real time and attracting some of our big clients like Paypal, Google, Forever 21, and Capitol Records.

When you get that domain name, don't worry about creating a website. You can easily just point the domain to your Facebook fan page for your business. You need to create these things ASAP. Forget about even doing a traditional website. We probably updated our website maybe once every six months, but we updated our social media accounts a few times a day. Especially when we were working on events for clients, we were constantly tweeting about their event with pictures and videos. Your website doesn't work in the same 'real-time' world as social media.

Social media is the easiest way to connect to an audience. You already have a built-in fan base, starting with your friends and family. You can update them right away. You can post pictures and client information. All of this can be done in real time, so you are constantly interacting and engaging with your audience.

If you don't have a social media presence, it's almost like you don't exist. I remember working with a vendor a few months ago, and when I first spoke with her, everything on the phone sounded great. I asked if she had a website, and she said, "No. It's something that I'm working on."

What? You said you've been doing this for twenty years and you don't have a website?!?

I searched for her company on Google, and I couldn't find any information at all. She said the company had done xyz and repre-sented this person and that person. I could only find one online article about it (maybe), but no social media, no website, nothing.

As much as I loved this person on the phone, I was very hesitant to do business with her company because it did not have a social media presence. Actually, it didn't have an internet presence at all, and in the 21st century, you have to. Because that's how people do commerce these days, that's how consumers validate your business and decide to spend money with you. Customers want to see what's going on. If you don't have a web presence, you are invisible.

We had built our business solely on those two platforms: Facebook and Twitter. There are thousands of social media networks out there. Facebook and Twitter may not be the ones that are best for you, but trust me, they are the ones that are usually best for your customers. There are others that you can tap into that are industry-specific as well. Before you do anything, get your social media presence up ASAP because it is the best way to connect with customers immediately.

7 Use and abuse Google docs.

Google docs is great for managing your team, and it's absolutely free. Software can be expensive and so can file storage. And, of course, you can't beat free! Google docs is great for collaborating on documents and projects with your team or vendors. You can also create forms and surveys that you can send to your clients when doing market research and product development.

8 Processing credit cards.

Whether you provide a service or you have a product, if you have a legitimate business in the 21st century, you need to process credit cards. These days, resources for you to process credit cards are either absolutely free or charge a very low monthly rate. If you want to be taken seriously and want to attract big customers, you have to be able to take credit cards. Most importantly, if you want to be paid ASAP, you need to take credit cards.

Paypal.com or Square.com (Square Up) are great resources for accepting credit cards. QuickBooks is connected to Intuit now, so you can take care of your credit cards within your invoicing system. It helps with the cash flow because you'll have that money available to you within a few short days.

9 **Learn how to leverage technology and delegation.** No man is an island! There will come a point when you have to delegate responsibilities and keep yourself and your team productive. You can get pretty creative in the process. Look into creating, building, and nurturing a virtual team whenever possible—this is the best thing you can do on a Ramen Noodle budget. Many small businesses are run out of a home office. But if your business is home-based and you need help, you may not have the space for employees to come to work every day.

Since we now live, work, and play in a virtual world, it is highly possible to hire a complete staff spread out all over the country or even in opposite corners of the world!

Automation is another friend of anyone looking to start a business on a Ramen Noodle budget. If there are ways you can accomplish several tasks at once with the push of a button or the dialing of the phone, then make it happen. Utilize technology to its fullest—it may allow you to be able to run a one-man show without disrespecting the value of your own time.

Here are two quick examples to illustrate how easy it is to automate a part of your business for free online:

> **Hootsuite** is a social media management tool that puts your social media marketing efforts on autopilot. If you're not in a place yet where you can outsource your social media, then this is a great tool to consolidate all of your social media efforts.

Setting up a **Hootsuite** account is free, and you can connect all of your social media accounts.

- Facebook
- Instagram
- Twitter
- Pinterest
- LinkedIn
- Business blog
- And others

Rather than missing out on the marketing opportunity that social media can provide or let social media marketing eat up too much of your time, you can type one update and it automatically posts on all the social media accounts you've set up.

Other awesome platforms similar to Hootsuite:

- Buffer
- Sprout Social
- Everypost

RevRecorder is another automation tool that allows you to record your notes, articles, and even entire essays or books into an app on your phone. Then, with the press of a button, you can get a live person to transcribe it for you for as low as a dollar a minute. This has been great for me, because I am always on the go and constantly like to put content out into the world with articles and blog post. As you build your personal brand, you'll want to make sure you are constantly sharing resources that position you as an expert, and tools like this allow you to get things done more efficiently.

These are just two examples of the myriad technology options available to make your business as simple and easy to run as possible. They save you time and money but allow you to accomplish what you need to keep your business moving ahead.

When you learn how to leverage technology and delegation, you go from working in your business to working on your business. You can be the wearer of all the hats but never have the time to master any of them, or you can learn how to master your role as the boss and business owner and allow everyone else to play their roles in the company well.

As a business owner on a Ramen Noodle budget, staying on top of the creative stage of your business is vital to its success in the long run.

More Resources

It took me a long time to get to the point where I stopped complaining that I was missing deadlines because I couldn't clone myself to letting technology work for me by "outsourcing" my life! Think of all the little (and sometimes big) mundane tasks that absolutely need to get done but constantly pull you from working on your big vision and those big money calls, meetings, and deals.

So, here are some life/business hacks that have worked for me over the years.

Phone Answering Service: Ultimate life saver! First, I refuse to walk around with more than one phone, so, in the beginning, Google Voice was perfect for me. And, having a separate number for business calls that was also free—Winning!!! As our team ramped up, we moved to Grasshopper.com so that we could have multiple mailboxes and a professional greeting. But, if you are constantly on the go and can't always get to the phone, you may have some unhappy clients who find they get connected to your voicemail every time they call. Starting at around $239 a month, you can use Ruby Receptionist, which provides a live receptionist to answer your calls, take messages, forward calls to your cell, and make phone calls on your behalf—all while monitoring everything from an app. There are some cheaper alternatives out there, but I have used Ruby Receptionist for over a year, and its high level of customer services is worth every penny.

Cloud Storage: Seems like no matter what you do, you can never have enough storage for all of your clients' amazing pictures and videos. Or perhaps your deck (presentation app) is ridiculously too big, but you don't want to resize it because you need your client to see just how badass every pixel of your talent really is. Fret not, my friend! Although Google offers its Google Drive that provides a ton of space for free, Dropbox is still at the top of my list for its ease of use and relatively cheap monthly payment plans.

Cleaning Service: While this may not be necessary for your business, it does free up your time so that you can focus on your business. I've used and love Molly Maids, but I often found it hard to work around their schedule. "Handy" has a nice little handy app that allows you to schedule within 8 hours and add extras like doing laundry, cleaning windows and ovens, and even going to the dry cleaners—and best of all you can pay directly within the app. Remember: Your time is money, and if it takes you 3 hours on the weekend to clean up your home, that's 3 hours you could be putting towards catapulting your company!

Legal: LegalZoom.com is cool, and I'm sure you've seen and heard their commercials a zillion times, but, in my opinion, you may end up paying for information and templates and still have a lot of the leg work to do. I'm a fan of CourtBuddy, which is an app that allows you to hire attorneys based on your budget and your needs. No more sweating bullets thinking that a contract review is going to cost you a small fortune.

Office/Meeting Space: It's time, my friends, to graduate from Starbucks as your meeting location. Sure the coffee smells great, but no amount of side eye is going to stop the barista from noisily blending that Frappuccino while you are on a conference call. I love working out of a "WeWork" office. Their locations are practically everywhere, which is great because once you are a member in one location, you have access to their other locations throughout the world. But, if you are on an extreme Ramen Noodle budget, check out liquidspaces.com for office space starting at around $15 an hour. On that site, you can find conference rooms and meeting spaces all around the United States. And, if you really have time to dig, you may even find free space.

create an
EXPERIENCE
or your business
WILL DIE!

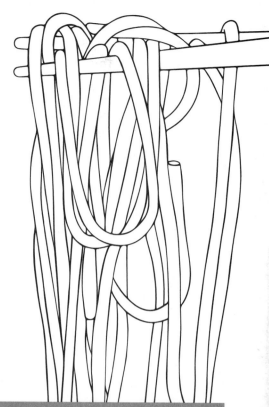

Chapter 6

No One Wants a Boring Noodle!

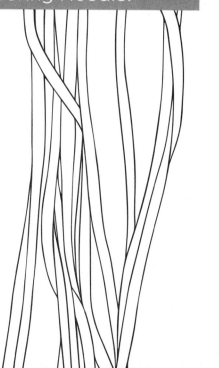

Chapter 6
No One Wants a Boring Noodle!

Why fit in, when you were born to stand out.

~Dr. Seuss

A few years ago, I wrote an article for the website Under30CEO.com titled, "The 5 Marketing Lessons That Young Entrepreneurs Can Learn from Nicki Minaj". I know what you're thinking . . . the rapper with the crazy hair colors? Yes, her! The main reason I wrote that article was because I was traveling and speaking at high schools, and I noticed so many girls sitting in my workshops who had hot pink hair or streaks of hot pink, bright purple, or bright blue hair. Nicki Minaj is in L.A., and girls in small towns in South Georgia were emulating her. You can't help but take notice.

That's when I thought, there are some really valuable marketing lessons that we can learn from not just her, but from lots of celebrities. Building a niche is all about standing out. The simple marketing lesson: if you can't be number one or number two in an industry, you need to create an industry that you *can* be number one in.

In the beverage industry, who is number one? Coca-Cola. But what about number two? Pepsi. What about number 7 or 13 or number 111? Do you know? Of course not! Do you even care? Coca-Cola and Pepsi have the world blanketed with their acidic products. It's going to be nearly impossible to break through as number one in the beverage industry. If you are a new beverage like Red Bull, how do you stand out? Red Bull is a beverage just like Pepsi, Coca-Cola, Sprite, milk, and water, but why does it stand out? Simple—its creators started a new industry called "energy drinks." Now who makes the number one energy drink? Red Bull. Do you see my point? You have to figure out the exact same thing for your business.

When we were starting our company, I knew we wanted to be different. There were tons of ice cream trucks that drove around the neighborhood and event companies that specifically targeted kids. The big niche for us was targeting adults with sophisticated flavors, as well as creating a design on our carts and trucks that would fit seamlessly into a fashion event, corporate event, wedding, or upscale party. Mixing nostalgia and indulgent dessert made us stand out. That's what you need to do.

We were not the number one ice cream truck in South Florida, but we were the number one adult gourmet pops company in South Florida and we were the top gourmet popsicle company in South Florida. Do you see where I'm going?

You also have to be unique. That is what will get you tons of free PR and clients screaming and knocking down your door, because when they think of you, your service, or your industry, you are at the top of their minds. You become synonymous with your industry. You are the one who they go to (or at least consider first) because you are number one. Once again, if you can't be number one or number two, you need to create your own industry that you can be number one in.

Vanity Marketing

1. Vanity marketing is a type of marketing that allows companies to work together with the public to help boost their sales through crowdsourcing and/or personalizing their products with names and pop culture phrases that will connect with consumers.

There is a marketing trend that, while it may not be new, is starting to resurface with new products such as Reese's®, Jones Soda Co.®, OREO® cookies, crowdsourced flavors like Lay's® Chicken & Waffles potato chips, and Coke® bottles with names on the packaging.

2. Social Media has made us a bit self-absorbed, so people are obsessed with seeing themselves,

their name, and likeness in the media and being associated with big-name corporations. As a small business, that provides you huge opportunities to get creative and promote your platform.

OREO® allowed people to connect their social media and create their own flavored OREO® cookies at the SXSW conference in 2015. OREO® then took the most popular flavors, created them, and put them in supermarkets. The company tapped into the creativity of consumers using crowdsourcing—wrapped in a fun experience—to gather new product ideas. People are obsessed with seeing themselves in the media and being associated with major corporations, and this equates to millions of dollars in sales for a brand like OREO®—and most importantly, the company was able to reengage consumers who had been ignoring its product.

The most lucrative part of our business model with Feverish Pops was allowing corporations to wrap our carts with their branding and were paid to do so. While not all consumers may know the Feverish Pops name, these larger corporations do. It provided the "vanity" that smaller businesses need so that their product becomes a commercial item for the larger brand. Any small business has real estate that it can offer to large corporations, which allows the two to be aligned with each other. Many small businesses don't know the real estate they have to offer to get these larger companies excited about the many vanity marketing opportunities.

Here's another example: you probably had a lemonade stand when you were a kid. That's how most kids start businesses. Lemons, water, and sugar—on a hot day in South Florida, you'll make lots of dough! But let's talk about being unique.

In one picture, you have the traditional stand, where kids are selling lemonade for 25 cents a cup. In the other picture, you have mint lemonade, lime iced tea, and other specialty flavors. It's a really sophisticated approach to the same idea of a lemonade stand.

We can imagine the kids with their cute smiles selling their lemonade for 25 cents. But I guarantee, you would pay much more money for the other lemonade because of the package it's wrapped in. It's still the same sugar, water, and lemons in a cup full of ice (so you really don't get that much lemonade), but you will pay more for it because of the packaging and the branding behind it.

That's what building a niche is all about. It will help you charge a premium price for your Ramen Noodle business, but you need to spend time getting the marketing, packaging, and identity of the product or service right.

I was at an event with this unique lemonade stand. The sellers were using organic fruit and sold a glass for $6 each easily—and there was a huge line. It's all about a creative approach!

Picking Your Niche and Being UNIQUE!

Find a low-competition niche market to start. Above all, you have to be unique when starting your business. The main reason we were able to garner so much media attention with Feverish Ice Cream and get big clients is because it is a really creative company and a creative brand.

Ice pops have been around for forever, and ice cream has been around even longer. Our ice cream trucks and carts were used, but we graphic-wrapped a unique design around them that made them look super cool and excited customers. When you're thinking about starting your business, you don't necessarily have to create the next big thing. A lot of times you can revamp and revolutionize an industry that is already tried and true. Make it look a little bit different. Create a different mystique to it. When you get creative and dig deep to find a niche in your industry, you'll be able to create or find a new audience that the industry has not yet been able to tap into.

"Show Me the Money!"

The second important thing when building a niche is, of course, raising the money. Sure, you're starting on a Ramen Noodle budget, but with the onslaught of all the crazy social media sites, you can tap into your network to raise money for your business in the form of something that is called . . . *crowdfunding*.

You probably know about *crowdsourcing*, which is reaching out to social networks to get people's opinions and their insight to help you with a decision or your product or idea. We do it all the time when we post a question to our friends on Facebook or Twitter. "Yo, what shirt do you think is better?" "What movie should I watch this weekend?" Or, "I am in Portland, what restaurant is the best?" That's called crowdsourcing. You're sourcing the crowd for opinions, information, and insight.

You can do the same thing to raise money for your business. Think of the pitch competitions or business plan competitions that are available for college students and adults starting their business or seeking a loan from the government, your bank, or the Small Business Association (SBA). Most people will put all their eggs in one basket trying to raise this money. "I'm going to apply for a $25,000 loan from one institution." Then, later you hear, "I didn't get it. I'm discouraged. I'm going to quit and check out of life." Oh my gosh!

But think about it, with crowdfunding, you can get 25,000 people to donate $1. That's still $25,000, and it sometimes takes less work than hitting up the bank!

That's the beauty of websites like Indiegogo.com, Kickstarter.com, Peerbackers.com, Crowdfunder.com, and Kiva.org (which is a micro-lending website). There are many crowd-funding platforms out there, where complete strangers (or even your family and friends) will give small donations to help you with your business.

I'll give a few examples. The first example is Issa Rae, a woman who started the web series, *Misadventures of the Awkward Black Girl*. She was a screenwriter, and, like many in her profession, she was frustrated that her show ideas were not being picked up by any of the major networks. So she decided to just start a comedy web series herself, with money from her own pocket! Starting at a super-low budget, she convinced friends to work as actors or in production jobs for almost nothing.

The videos appeared on Issa Rae's website and YouTube and started getting a crazy following. Right now, the web shows get about 300,000 views each. Insane! So when she ran out of money and wanted to complete the rest of the season, she put up a campaign on Kickstarter.com. She set a goal of $30,000 and tapped into her network of fans who absolutely love the show and want to support her.

The campaign lasted about two months, and it raised $50,000 from small donations from fans to continue that season and even go into a second season of filming. Complete strangers—but people who absolutely loved her product and loved her shows—contributed to the success of raising the money to keep it going. Issa Rae currently has a deal with Shonda Rimes, who created *Grey's Anatomy*, *Private Practice*, and *Scandal*, to develop a show for NBC. Can we all say Epic!!!

Traditional thinking would have said to wait around, try to get a loan, or just keep shopping the show around for years hoping any network will pick it up. The new way of doing things: Create your own opportunity. Create a profile with a high-quality and compelling video. Reach out to strangers, your fans, and your network, and use technology to raise $50,000. It worked for Issa Rae!

Another example is a vegan food truck in South Florida. The owners were about $10,000 short on the money they needed in order to finish their food truck. So, they did the same thing. They posted an ad on Facebook saying that they needed people to help raise money. For every $50 you donated, you would get $50 back in food credit. It was ingenious. Of course, they ended up opening their truck and raising a ton of money to do so. You've got to get creative with the approach. Get people engaged and involved in what you're doing.

When the campaign started, the food truck owners were already in operation, so they were able to raise money and make good on their promise of credit for food. Another word for this is pre-sales. A pre-sale is a great way to offer something that is not going to take too much away from your bottom line, while getting people excited, engaged, and passionate about your cause. There are a lot of people who want to help young entrepreneurs. They may not have tons of money, but they do have $50, or $100, or even a few thousand bucks to give to a cause. Crowdfunding is a great way to raise money for your business.

More About Pre-Sales

Another approach is to start taking orders to try out your business model and make sure it works. When I was a little kid in elementary school and we were fundraising for our school, we would walk around before Christmas with a little catalog selling popcorn in a tin and wrapping paper. Mind you, we were walking around going door-to-door with a catalog. What did our neighbors do? If they liked the samples, they placed orders and gave me their money. Then, six weeks later, they would receive their order in the mail.

So, pre-sales are another great way to raise money for your business. You get cash flow and the money that you need for your expenses to make the product ahead of time. You don't even need to purchase a garage full of inventory, just sell the product in advance, taking orders for later delivery. You make the product as the orders come in and start with the money you need to cover your costs. Ingenious!

You can only live on
potential for so long ...

there will come a time when
people will require you to
cash in on that potential,

and, at that time,
your potential must
produce profits.

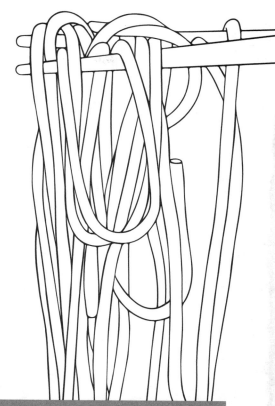

Chapter 7

Hey, Even Ramen Noodles Cost Money!

Chapter 7
Hey, Even Ramen Noodles Cost Money!

"Money is like gasoline during a road trip. You don't want to run out of gas on your trip, but you're not doing a tour of gas stations."

-Tim O'Reilly, O'Reilly Media founder and CEO

One thing that *is* true, you must get creative to start your business on a Ramen Noodle budget. In this chapter, we are going to discuss some ways to stretch your noodles so you can grow your business.

For example, if you're starting a marketing consulting business from your home or dorm room, you may already have the equipment you need to start the business: a phone, computer, internet access, and printer. With no rent payment due each month for office space, you may only need to cover your phone and internet service. Now that's what I call starting a business on a Ramen Noodle budget!

Sources of Funding

Once you know how much money you need to start your business and how much money you need to cover the operating costs of the business for six to twelve months, then it's time to determine where you can pull this money from.

Crowdfunding

Crowdfunding is a great and creative way to get fans, family and friends interested in your products to help you raise money online. The Vegan Food Truck and Issa Rae are great examples of how effective this source of funding can be. Thanks to social media and faster and more widespread technology than ever before, crowdfunding is a game changer.

How would you like to raise money by getting someone else to do the work for you? That's what crowdfunding offers. Up until fairly recently, crowdfunding was actually dramatically limited by U.S. securities regulations, but with the JOBS (Jumpstart Our Business Startups) Act now in place, businesses are entitled to raise up to $1 million from 1,000 investors, as long as no single investor owns more than 10% of the business. And, under the new law, the business is exempt from general securities legislation.

Entrepreneurs now have the power to raise money through the internet and social media. Let's do a short crash course in crowdfunding your new business!

As previously discussed, crowdfunding is a method of finding startup investors using the internet. Entrepreneurs create a business proposal that is showcased on a crowdfunding website, allowing visitors—the "crowd"—to view the proposal and invest money if they're interested. Before the JOBS Act, crowdfunding was allowed for pure gifts of cash to new ideas, as in Issa Rae's story, or for pre-sales, as in the example of the food truck.

But now, with the JOBS Act, investors are able to either receive a stake in the company (less than 10%) or a return on the investment. That is the new innovation. And I believe that in the coming years, we will see what an incredible opportunity this is for small businesses (and investors!) everywhere!

Let's explore a number of crowdfunding platforms, success stories from the crowdfunding world, and steps you can take to create your own successful crowdfunding project.

First, let's discuss crowdfunding platforms and strategies.

Crowdfunding Platforms

Kickstarter

Kickstarter is a crowdfunding platform launched in 2009, and it has quickly grown into the most popular crowdfunding website, launching over 60,000 projects and raising over $237 million. Kickstarter's founders set things up so there is both a funding goal and a deadline. Kickstarter then uses an "all-or-nothing" approach: you must raise your goal amount by the deadline, or the funds will not be collected from investors and passed along to you.

Kickstarter Pros and Cons

Size: The biggest advantage to using Kickstarter is size. It is the largest crowdfunding site on the internet by far, and it has the most interest from potential investors. This interest can increase your chances of raising money. However, the popularity of Kickstarter can be a double-edged sword, as you will be competing for attention with many other projects on the platform.

Project Types: Kickstarter has a relatively strict approval process for projects; they must be creative in nature. In addition, Kickstarter focuses heavily on the arts, media, and inventions. Kickstarter rejects up to 40% of project proposals.

IndieGogo

IndieGogo is a platform that is older than Kickstarter; it was created in 2008. Like Kickstarter, IndieGogo projects create a proposal page and set a fundraising goal and timeline. The difference is that IndieGogo projects will receive any funds raised even if they don't meet their fundraising goal.

IndieGogo Pros and Cons

Less Restrictive on Projects: Unlike Kickstarter, IndieGogo allows any legal business proposals to be entered on the platform—even a charitable cause. However, this freedom can also be a drawback, as your project will be competing with a wide range of projects from professional to frivolous, making it challenging to be heard above the noise.

Keep Any Raised Funds: This policy allows for a lower risk in starting a project on IndieGogo, as you may still keep the funds you raise even if you don't meet your goal; however, an all-or-nothing goal can potentially be a powerful motivational tool.

Microventures

Microventures is a more formal service than IndieGogo and Kickstarter. Started in 2010, it serves as a broker between startups and investors. Founders submit a business plan that goes through an application process and due diligence. Microventures then handles the raising of startup money through its network of angel investors, usually raising between $100,000 and $500,000.

Microventures Pros and Cons

Suited for Tech Companies: Microventures specializes in startups in the technology space. Because of this specialization, this service can provide far more in-depth business support than a general crowdfunding platform.

Rigorous Process: The approval and due-diligence process makes Microventures one of the most selective crowdfunding processes on the market, and chances of approval can be slim. However, this process serves as great training for creating business plans that will serve well when looking for additional funding in the future.

Rockethub

Rockethub was started in 2010, and it offers a very similar service to that of Kickstarter and IndieGogo. Like IndieGogo, Rockethub allows folks to keep all raised funds even if they do not achieve their targeted fundraising goal.

Rockethub Pros and Cons

Support for Beginners: Rockethub is aiming to simplify crowdfunding for beginners by introducing its own terminology and providing an achievement system for motivating founders to complete fundraising tasks.

Lack of Size: Rockethub offers a very similar service to that of IndieGogo, but is far smaller, meaning there are far fewer potential investors for each project. Because of this, it's difficult to see what advantages Rockethub holds over these competing services.

Crowdfunder

Crowdfunder uses a similar model to Microventures; however, the approval process has a twist: startups compete in a contest to win funding.

Crowdfunder will operate much like Kickstarter in its second phase, where approved ventures will have a profile page to promote themselves, develop interest, and raise funds. Since the JOBS Act went into effect in 2013, the site is a platform, meaning it can process crowdfunding investments in the new way, with either equity or returns for the investors, not just donations and pre-sales.

Crowdfunder Pros and Cons

Solid Advisory Panel: Crowdfunder has collected a panel of entrepreneurial professionals to act as contest judges and also provide advisory support; this is a compelling benefit for novice entrepreneurs looking to learn from experienced thought leaders.

Crowdfunding Success Stories

Pebble

Pebble is the most successful Kickstarter project to date, having raised over $10 million from over 68,000 backers. It is an e-ink smart watch, using the same technology used in e-readers to create a watch with a unique look and smart features like customized apps.

Why Pebble Was Successful

Cool Technology: Pebble founder Eric Migicovsky says the technology was central to the project's success. The Pebble watch uses existing technologies in a novel way, creating a watch that is unique, yet it has many of the covetable qualities of great tech products like the Apple iPhone.

A Relatable Pitch: While the technology of the product is unique, Migicovsky was careful to describe the product's benefits in a way that was relatable, using his mother as a test subject for his pitch. By making the product relatable, he ensured interest from the widest range of potential backers.

Amanda Palmer

Amanda Palmer was a relatively unknown musician from Boston who raised more than $1 million on Kickstarter to fund a new studio album. This is the highest funded music project on Kickstarter.

Why Amanda Was Successful

A Loyal Following: Though Amanda did not have a huge following, her fans are extremely loyal, and Amanda used many online channels to interact closely with her fans. This allowed her to promote the Kickstarter project and set the fundraising in motion.

Transparent with Her Backers: Amanda built credibility by explaining exactly how all of the money would be spent producing the album, even disclosing how much money she would keep for herself as payment.

FOLLOW YOUR

MOST **EPIC**

DREAMS

Coffee Joulies

Dave Petrillo and Dave Jackson created Coffee Joulies in 2011. They are stainless steel coffee bean–shaped stones that you put in your coffee to keep it comfortably warm for longer. Their Kickstarter project raised over $300,000.

Why Coffee Joulies Was Successful

Good Communication: When producing a physical product, production issues and team constraints can make meeting high demand a challenge. The Coffee Joulies team had a policy of open communication to allow investors a full view of when their product would be available.

Email List: As part of this communication policy, Coffee Joulies built an opt-in email list, which created a powerful marketing channel to drive more sales.

Satarii Star

Satarii Star is an example of a successful IndieGogo project that launched in February 2011. This motion-tracking camera accessory raised over $24,000—over 125% of the fundraising goal.

Why Satarii Star Was Successful

Compelling Pitch Video: The Satarii Star proposal included a pitch video that was hosted on YouTube, receiving over 500,000 views. This compelling content was highly shared and drew a lot of traffic to the IndieGogo proposal.

Coverage in Tech Media: The Satarii Star proposal was also featured in a number of online technology publications, including Engadget, Techcrunch, and Gizmodo. This coverage drove over 10,000 comments and emails regarding the IndieGogo project.

Shopobot

Shopobot is an example of a successful Microventures project. Founded in 2011, it is a website that uses price trackers and social media to recommend products when the price is low. Shopobot successfully completed a $150,000 funding round with Microventures.

Why Shopobot Was Successful

Solid Business Plan: Unlike Kickstarter or IndieGogo, Microventures projects go through an intense due diligence process, which means a business plan must be created.

Projects that successfully pass the due diligence scrutiny must have a well-crafted business plan.

Credible Founders: As part of the funding round, Shopobot founders Julius Schorzman and Dave Matthews had to personally complete a conference call to answer questions from potential investors. Founders must establish credibility with investors quickly to assure the soundness of an investment.

How to Achieve Crowdfunding Success

While each of the previous crowdfunding examples had notable reasons for success, in reality, crowdfunding projects succeed due to a combination of many factors. Here are a few strategic steps to maximize your chances of crowdfunding success:

Choose the Right Platform

The crowdfunding platform that you choose can have a serious effect on the success of your project. The popularity of Kickstarter is incredibly advantageous, making it a compelling option if your project qualifies. If it doesn't qualify for Kickstarter, try out IndieGogo. If you have a tech idea that would qualify for Microventures, then investigate that platform. Look at the projects that have achieved success on the platform, and decide whether success for your project seems plausible.

Be Authentic

Successful crowdfunding founders are passionate and authentic. In many ways, crowdfunding is an underdog story, providing funding to people that big banks and investors might pass over. Crowdfunding backers are investing in the founder as much as the business idea, so let your personality come through in your proposal. Introduce yourself, and communicate why you feel your project idea is important. Instead of showing why your product will be lucrative, show how your product will make the world a better place. Be open and communicative with your backers.

Create a Compelling Pitch

A common factor in every successful project is a compelling pitch, and for almost all crowdfunding projects, this pitch comes in the form of an online video. A pitch video has the advantage of being easy to watch, compared to reading pages of text, and it's easy to share, an important factor in allowing your project to go viral. Watch other successful viral videos to see what works, and model your pitch after those:

- Keep it short: ideally under 2 to 3 minutes.
- Showcase the product—and yourself; authenticity is key.
- Keep the production value high, and make it look professional.
- Make it compelling enough to share.

A good way to develop an eye for these factors is to watch the pitch videos from successful projects. Each of the successful examples discussed before had a great pitch video.

Provide Appealing Incentives to Invest

One of the most appealing features of crowdfunding is that many platforms allow investors to contribute as much or as little as they would like. This is to your advantage, as it allows you to gather support for your project even when a potential investor can't contribute much. Many crowdfunding platforms allow the founder to create rewards for investors. These are gifts that a backer receives in exchange for investing, and most platforms allow you to easily create tiered rewards, with bigger rewards offered for bigger contributions.

Create compelling reasons for investors to contribute. Start at $1, offering a personalized thank-you for backers; every dollar counts, and you certainly want to include every possible investor. This is also a great opportunity to add potential customers to your email list. At tiers from $5 to $25, think about offering branded merchandise, like t-shirts or mugs, provided they can be offered profitably. These serve a double purpose as both a reward and good marketing material for your project. The $25 tier is often the most popular investment level for backers. If you offer a physical product, this may be a good level at which to offer it, provided it fits your profit margins.

To attract even higher levels of investment, think about offering experiences that give a sense of inclusion in the project. For example, Amanda Palmer offered a private concert to backers who contributed over $300. Investors want to feel that they are an important part of the project, and experiences can count for a lot—offer a name credit if you are creating a media production, or make a personal phone call. Creative experiences can mean a lot to backers, and it can really drive investment to higher levels.

Actively Market Your Campaign

With the number of crowdfunding platforms and projects on the market, it is unlikely that people will stumble upon your project by accident. The first step in marketing your campaign is to create a base level of donations from your friends and family. Crowdfunding is a momentum-based process, and strangers will not invest in a project unless it already has credibility in the form of other investments. This means that you must be active in the first few days of your fundraising, getting donations on your page from everyone in your personal social network.

Once your project has a base level of donations, start marketing your pitch video with online publications, like blogs. Find blogs with high viewership in the area of your project, e.g. Techcrunch for technology. Many of these publications look for news stories on new ventures, and you have a good chance of getting coverage if your pitch video is compelling. Market your pitch video everywhere you can, from your personal Facebook network to social news sites like Reddit. Sharing your pitch in many relevant outlets will maximize your chances of the video being shared and traffic being driven to your proposal.

Other Sources of Capital

Banks

Loans from banks are another source of funds to start your business on a Ramen Noodle budget. This is the most common source of borrowed capital, and traditional sources will tell you it is your only option. While historically commercial banks have been the main source of small business loans, it is more common today for small businesses, especially those on a minimal budget, to turn to other types of banking institutions, such as community banks and credit unions.

The truth is that banks are not lending like they used to and now have more stringent guidelines and requirements that you must meet to obtain the loan, even if it is a small one. For example, most banks require first-time small business borrowers to invest at least 25 percent of their own funds.

Banks that lend startup money to small business owners want to see that you have your own resources and are willing to invest at least some of your own money into the business. In addition, most banks want your personal credit score to be high. Others may require that you have some kind of an asset to use as collateral for the loan.

If you do not have enough in cash savings, you may need to cut back spending in other areas of your life so that you have more money to funnel into the savings account for the business startup fund. Starting a business on a Ramen noodle budget is going to require you to sacrifice. As an entrepreneur, for a few years, you will have to live a life that most people are not willing to live in order to *then* live the life that most people can't live.

Friends and Family

Another source of funding, especially when raising money for a startup is the "Friends and Family" round of funding. This comes before the seed round, series A and series B. Some business experts suggest that you draw the line between your business ventures and your personal life, but friends and family members can offer you a loan with much better terms than a typical small business bank loan will offer you. Some may even consider it an investment of their money; you can pay them back when and if the business takes off.

If you would rather keep it on a business level, draw up a formal contract, where you pay interest on the money you borrow. The interest rate on the loan still tends to be lower than the going rate at the bank, so at least you can obtain the funds you need and keep the overall cost down to a minimum.

Go over your plan with your friends and family members just as you would with a bank that considers lending you money. It's important that they understand where their money is going and what you expect to do with your business.

Factoring/Leasing Companies

If you're starting a business on a Ramen Noodle budget that requires special equipment or machinery, then leasing companies tend to be a good option for obtaining the equipment you need. Rather than spending cash up front to outright purchase the machines and equipment or borrow the money to buy the equipment, you can lease the equipment instead.

Some of the items available for leasing include office furniture, vehicles, trucks, computers, and production or manufacturing machinery. The leasing company is the owner of the item, but it allows you to use the item in exchange for a monthly payment. Some leases have the option to purchase, while others simply have you return the item to the leasing company when your lease comes to an end.

The main benefit is that you can save on the money you spend upfront. The second main benefit of leasing is flexibility because it gives you access to the items you need to operate your business for the time that you need them (short-term).

Private Investors

Venture Capital (VC) vs. Angel Investors? It's all the buzz with tech startups. Private investors are another option for funding your business when you're on a Ramen Noodle budget. For the most part, private investors will want an ownership interest in your business, so you would be paying them a percentage of your profits once the business starts to turn a profit. You may be able to find private investors by attending local startup events or national events like SXSW in Austin, Texas. Your tax advisor and business attorney are another set of matchmakers between business owners looking to launch a business and investors who are interested in putting their money to good use.

Something else to consider before taking on investors . . .

You need more than money!!!

It's so easy to get wowed by the money. You will need more than just money, and sometimes you will find that you don't really need money at all. Be clear: express your needs to your investor, and determine what resources and doors your partners can open for you—or if they can open those doors at all. The right partner should be able to not only assist you financially but also help with resources that will accelerate growth for your business. They are there to help make sure that your business is a success. So, be clear on exactly what you need from them to help your business win big.

Want to know more about my experience taking on investors in our business? Read more online here http://tinyurl.com/FeleciaInvestorAdvice.

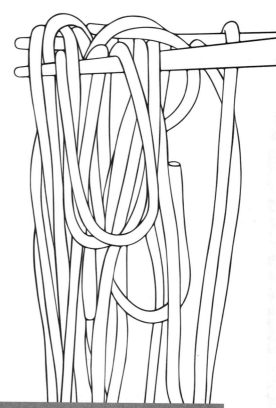

Chapter 8

Every Noodle Has a Story

Chapter 8

Every Noodle Has a Story

> "The reason I think storytelling is the most underrated skill in business is because it doesn't get talked about a whole lot, and I don't think people realize it's happening when it's happening, and most of all, I don't think that many people are really good at it..."

~Gary Vaynerchuk, CEO, Wine Library TV and Vaynermedia

Storytelling in Business

Some of the most powerful and longstanding ideas in our culture started their life as stories. Storytelling and the oral tradition have been around almost as long as humans have used spoken language. Stories are such a natural part of everyday communication that we often don't notice their prevalence and power. Almost everyone, regardless of background or culture, has grown up with stories being the backbone of learning new ideas. It should come as no surprise that many of the most successful marketers in the business world have harnessed the power of story.

Storytelling in business is an effective force for allowing ideas to spread in a meaningful, authentic way. Here we will explore the types of stories that can be used in business, look at cases of people and organizations that have used storytelling successfully, and discuss ways that storytelling can be used in your own business ventures.

Types of Storytelling

Brand Story

Origin stories are an important phenomenon both in history and in popular culture. A brand story can be thought of as the origin story of your company, and it should be one of the first things you consider as you begin your marketing efforts. A brand story succinctly expresses the reason why your company is in business. It ties a narrative thread between what your company stands for, its values, and what traits your brand has developed to represent those core values and beliefs.

Why a Brand Story Is Important

A brand story should be one of your first marketing efforts because it helps to crystallize not just the message you send to others, but the core of your company's identity internally. By framing the origin of your brand as a story, you create a mythology that all your marketing efforts can build upon. You can also use this story to help communicate your internal strategy, to express your core principles to your employees in a way that can be easily shared and subscribed to within your company.

Product Story

Once the origin and direction of your company has been framed as a story, it becomes easier to look at each individual product offering as its own story or "chapter" in your book. Products are supposed to solve a problem in the life of the user. By expressing this drama as a story, you create a memorable and compelling way to succinctly express the benefits and value of your offering.

Why a Product Story Is Important

People don't become passionate about a product by simply hearing a list of its benefits or features. People develop passion by seeing how the product fits into the narrative of their everyday lives, making their lives easier or more pleasurable. A story can illustrate the benefits of a product, but it should do so in a way that is impactful, compelling, and far more likely to be shared. Tell a story of how your product will be used, and the listeners will instinctively picture themselves using it—making your product's benefits more tangible and personal to your audience.

Infographics

Business and society are moving toward a data-driven culture every day. As we continue to develop our ability to collect data using technology, customers and companies alike are increasingly using data to make decisions. Despite this growing reliance on data, human beings are still only able to process a finite amount of information at a time. Showing customers too much data can be an easy way to overwhelm them, and your message can get lost. Infographics are a recent trend that has sought to solve this problem. They are a mixture of art and science, aimed at presenting data in a way that is visually engaging and succinctly explaining the meaning behind the data points.

Why Infographics Are Important

Data almost always tells a story, but sometimes it's hard to find the narrative when presented with a mass of unstructured charts and numbers. Presenting data on its own forces readers to draw their own conclusions, and sometimes those conclusions can be unclear. An infographic allows you to map out the story and present supporting data in a way that maximizes its impact, and it allows you to craft the message and use the data to add credibility and legitimacy to your message.

Explainer Videos

A compelling way to tell a product story that has become increasingly popular is the explainer video. While many companies have created compelling brand or product stories, presenting these stories as plain text on a website almost guarantees it to be skimmed over by many potential customers. The explainer video presents the value proposition of a product or service in a way that is succinct, engaging, and far more likely to be shared.

Why Explainer Videos Are Important

With more and more startups and crowdfunded projects arising every day, it becomes difficult to present a new product in a way that will be heard above the din of competition. A video that explains the story of a product will capture the attention of your customers far better than presenting a long narrative in text, and, if your video is compelling and innovative enough, it may be shared virally. This can turn your customers into one of your most valuable marketing allies via word of mouth. A well-made video explaining your product can be more impactful than pages of written benefits, value propositions, and data.

Examples of Storytelling in Business

Gary Vaynerchuk

Gary Vaynerchuk has become an advocate for the importance of storytelling in business, and his commitment to storytelling infuses his own narrative as a businessman. As the son of a liquor store owner, Gary developed a passion for wine and a vision for making wine accessible to the middle-class American consumer. He started Wine Library TV, a series of video and social media initiatives aimed at bringing wine to the masses. Over time, his passion and engagement with fans grew the brand into a huge success. The Wine Library flagship store now eclipses the old site of his father's liquor store, and Vaynerchuk has authored a number of best-selling books on harnessing passion in business.

Why Gary Vaynerchuk Was Successful

Weaving the Narrative Throughout: Vaynerchuk ended every Wine Library TV broadcast with the tagline "You, with a little bit of me, we're changing the wine world, whether they like it or not." This one sentence is itself the backbone of a story. It has the protagonists, the antagonists, and the struggle. This story was infused into all of the efforts of Wine Library and became the rallying cry for all of the fans who engaged with the brand.

Make the Story Personal: As you can see from the tagline, Vaynerchuk wanted the customer, the viewer, to become as much a part of the story as he was. Together, they would take on the wine world, and Vaynerchuk made sure to foster this togetherness by engaging with his fans. As Wine Library was on the rise, Vaynerchuk answered every email and tweet from his fans, engaging through all forms of social media and making sure his fans felt that they, too, were an important part of the Wine Library story.

Flipboard

Flipboard is an iPad application that aims to change the way we engage with blogs and online media. Flipboard combs through all of the latest blogs, collects posts grouped by various subjects, and presents them in a magazine format on the iPad that someone can flip through and browse in an engaging way. Flipboard is a great example of a company that used an explainer video with great success. Their product video, entitled "Meet Flipboard," has been viewed over 700,000 times, and the app has met with both critical and commercial success.

Why Flipboard Was Successful

A Succinct Explainer Video: The explainer video "Meet Flipboard" is not even 90 seconds long—it takes just 1 minute and 20 seconds to explain the product. A short, engaging explainer video can capture and hold a viewer's attention far easier than a video that belabors the features and benefits of the product. Attention spans in the internet age are short, and Flipboard recognized this to good effect.

Showed a User with the Product: "Meet Flipboard" showed a user casually using the product and connecting with friends. Viewers could easily visualize themselves using the product and being a part of the product's story. Explainer videos that create this personal connection to the narrative can make a strong impact and engagement with customers.

Steve Jobs' Keynotes

Steve Jobs became world renowned as the charismatic leader of Apple and the face of its landmark product launches. Keynote addresses given by Jobs ascended to almost mythical status in the tech world as being fitting introductions to world-changing products. Many marketing experts agree that much of Jobs' impact as a presenter was due to his masterful ability as a storyteller.

Why Steve Jobs' Keynotes Were Successful

A Strong, Short Headline: Many traditional stories begin with the iconic words "Once upon a time . . ." Steve Jobs looked to harness iconic headlines to set up his own narratives. He distilled his product story into a few simple words—the product usually appeared alone on one slide, and he would return to that during the course of his presentation. These short headlines created a lasting impact in the mind of the viewer.

Fight a Villain: The center of almost all stories is a struggle, and Steve Jobs was well known for characterizing this struggle by creating a villain. In the early days of Apple, these villains were IBM and Microsoft. Later on, they became ideas like outdated notions of buying music or interacting with phones. Jobs created drama in his stories by always showing the audience what Apple, and Apple's customers, were up against.

KISSmetrics

KISSmetrics is a web analytics service that allows website owners to track their audience's behavior. This is a highly data-driven business, and recognizing this, KISSmetrics used infographics very successfully in its marketing efforts. The service created a series of over 30 infographics covering a variety of topics from the impact of different colors on websites to using video to increase website viewership. These infographics have been extremely popular and have been shared over social media hundreds of thousands of times.

Why KISSmetrics Was Successful

Engaging to the Eye: KISSmetrics uses a variety of colors and visual styles to ensure that its infographics display data in a way that is visually engaging to the reader. By mixing up styles, the company makes sure that the data doesn't become visually fatiguing, causing the reader to start skimming over important facts.

Make the Story Easy to Share: Each KISSmetrics infographic is presented on a separate page and has prominent buttons to share on Facebook, Twitter, LinkedIn, Google+, and Buffer. By making many sharing options readily available, KISSmetrics increases the likelihood that its messages will be shared and seen by others.

Dropbox

Dropbox is a startup company that has created an online storage solution to allow users to save and share their files over the web. Dropbox took a complex technical product and presented it in a compelling way, using a low-tech paper animation explainer video to highlight its benefits and uses.

Why Dropbox Was Successful

Make the Story Central: Dropbox created a fictional character "Josh," who was preparing for a trip through Africa. The video tells the story of Josh's trip and how he used Dropbox during his travels to keep his files safe and to share photos with his family.

Call to Action: The Dropbox front page is incredibly simple, consisting of just the video telling the product story and a large button to download Dropbox for free. The narrative in the video leads to a clear call to action to try the product for yourself, thus facilitating the opt-in process for the customer.

How to Use Storytelling in Your Business Stories

Have a Structure

While we encounter stories all the time, we often don't think critically about what makes a story different from other types of messages. Here are four structural elements to consider:

1. **Plot**—A definite beginning, middle, and end and a progression through each stage. Instead of a static description of things, stories are moving; they take the reader on a journey. Where do users of your product begin, physically and emotionally? Where do they end up?

2. **Character**—How are you engaging with your audience as the protagonist, and who (or what) are you up against? Can viewers of your story easily visualize themselves as the hero of your story?

3. **Drama**—The struggle in a business story is in desire versus danger. How do you and your company desire to change the world? What are the dangers that threaten this desire?

4. **An Idea**—Your product or service is the idea, the secret weapon that's going to allow you to win in the end. How will your product accomplish this?

Tell the Truth

Authenticity is an extremely important aspect of any marketing message. Savvy, connected consumers are very sensitive to being misled, now more so than ever before. Even if you are presenting a fictional or hypothetical scenario, you must resist the urge to overtly persuade with your story. A story that presents your product or service in a realistic way, and has a ring of truth to it, will be far more compelling than any pure fiction. Audiences can easily tell when a story is based on truth and will gravitate toward truthfulness with their tastes. When I first started Feverish, I was embarrassed to tell people that I came up with the idea for the company because I fell while chasing after an ice cream truck in heels. Now when I share that story, people have an instant connection to it. Our story humanized Feverish.

Trim the Detail

Using the example of both Flipboard and Dropbox, keep your story short. Explainer videos, in particular, rarely need to be longer than 2 minutes in length and are often more impactful when they are shorter. Stories in general suffer when they become too long; nobody likes having to listen to a story that's overstayed its welcome. Look at every detail of your stories, and make a frank assessment of whether that detail absolutely needs to be included. Work with a desire to tell your full story in the shortest way possible.

Make It Personal

Like Gary Vaynerchuk, make sure you engage with your audience and include them as part of the narrative. Stories are most impactful when we are able to involve ourselves as part of the drama. Remind your audience that you are taking a journey together, and use examples, like product demonstrations in explainer videos that easily allow audience members to visualize themselves using and benefitting from your product.

Give Your Audience an Idea—Invite Them to Dream

Steve Jobs' presentations were often impactful because they left the viewers with an idea, a vision of the future that was made better by Apple's groundbreaking products. This instilled a desire in the audience to help create this future by buying the product. End your stories with an idea, or vision; make it general, not too specific. Allow the audience to fill in some of the blanks by inserting their own desires into this vision, thus creating engagement. End your stories by showing the world of possibilities that your product or brand creates. This is the "happily ever after" idea. By creating this vision, you invite your audience to turn the story into a reality by engaging with your brand.

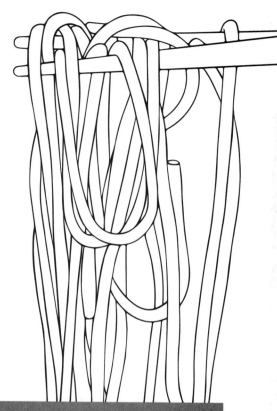

Chapter 9

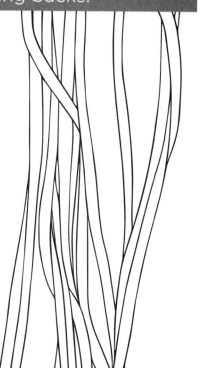

Your Advertising Sucks!

Chapter 9
Your Advertising Sucks!

"You can buy attention (advertising). You can beg for attention from the media (PR). You can bug people one at a time to get attention (sales). Or you can earn attention by creating something interesting and valuable and then publishing it online for free."

– David Meerman Scott,
Marketing Strategist — www.davidmeermanscott.com

The best advertising is word of mouth. The tools that amplify your word of mouth best today are social media and great public relations. The best way to facilitate word of mouth is to sell **HIGH-QUALITY** products that are buzzworthy. Always work to sell something that people will want to talk about positively.

Media Attention

As I mentioned earlier, Feverish Ice Cream has received a lot of media attention for free. When we were featured on NBC's *Today Show* at 8:30 a.m., the 2-minute segment was comparable to $1.5 million in advertising. That's insane, right? It didn't cost us anything except for a few hours of our time over the course of two days. There are still people who come down to Florida on vacation and track down Feverish Ice Cream because they saw us on the Cooking Channel or the *Today Show*.

So, you see, there are other ways to advertise your business that do not have to cost a fortune.

Become the Go-To Person in Your Niche

What's in a profile and what's in a name? Let me show you the power of a name. How do you feel when you hear that my job title is not CEO but the Chief Popsicle? When customers hear that or see that on a business card they instantly laugh or smile, and it's a conversation starter right off the bat. We were even featured in an article by Dow Jones & Company's "Market Watch" called, "Chief Popsicle: How a cool job title spurs success."

Brand Equity

Have you ever asked yourself why some people prefer to go to McDonald's over some mom-and-pop burger joint? It's because they feel somewhat assured of the consistency and familiarity they're going to get if they go to a McDonald's anywhere around the world. The power of a name affects customer behavior.

The brand name McDonald's is valued at $81.1 billion and is currently ranked 11th in the world's most valuable brands. $81.1 billion is the price any company wishing to acquire McDonald's will have to pay, for the name alone. It took McDonald's years of operations, advertising, and effectively satisfying its customers day in and day out to get to this status. This $81.1 billion is the value of their brand equity. *(Source: Statista.com)*

The purpose of building your profile is to generate brand equity for yourself. Brand equity is the power of a brand that produces marketing leverage, and, in this case, your name. If you want to create a nice brand name for your portfolio aside from your own name, by all means go for it. If you do consider a brand name, however, make sure to copyright it. You don't want to spend your time and energy building a brand only for it to be used by someone else later.

Building your Reputation

Free but effective ways to build your reputation include:

- Make sure your web page tells a compelling story about you. Keep it simple, factual, and organized. People connect with vivid stories that really paint a picture. (We talked about storytelling in Chapter 8.)

- Create blogs outside of your webpage. This can potentially drive traffic to your website, too; for example, blogging has been way more effective for Feverish than its website.

- Create profiles on social networking sites like Facebook, Twitter, and LinkedIn. Network with lots of "friends." Make sure your page is always updated, and be sure to announce interesting things once in a while. Motivational quotes and memes are usually great ways to engage your audience and create traction.

- Get featured in a local magazine or newspaper. Do not shy away from interviews. Free resources to connect with journalists like HARO (www.HelpaReporter.com), SourceBottle.com, and www.PitchRate.com make it easy to connect with journalists. Our company has been featured on ABCnews.com, on NBC, in *Inc. Magazine,* and in the *Wall Street Journal Japan* because of connections on HARO. These are media alerts that go out two to three times a day when journalists are looking for people to interview for their stories for radio, TV, newspapers, and the Web.

- Offer free classes in your niche if you can. You gain friends, you gain fans, you gain popularity, and you become the go-to person in your niche! This is great for building a personal brand. Building a personal brand helps to expand your message and gain credibility as an expert in your industry.

- Do volunteer work. Charity work is one of the most effective ways to build your reputation as a socially responsible

person. If you use your passion as the means to support a
charity, you gain patronage. Your business is not just about
earning money. It has a cause to support, and you help
people and make this world a better place.

- Join associations and do not be afraid to accept leadership
positions. When you lead, you develop management skills
and become better at working with people. Leading devel-
ops charisma, and charismatic people attract a following.

- Write an ebook and give it away for free. Being able to write
a book builds your creditbility as an expert in that field. It
also serves as a permanent business card. People throw
business cards away all the time, but they'll place a book on
their coffee table or bookshelf forever.

Building your name is a continuous endeavor and one that will constantly require you to update your skills in order to become the preferred
go-to person in your niche. Develop public speaking skills. Be generous.
Give out free samples. Volunteer if you can. Start a crusade. Always be
dependable. Join clubs or associations, and accept leadership positions.

Building your personal brand name is one of the best strategies, and
while it may take some time, it's more than worth it in the end. Remember:
a reputation isn't built overnight, but once you have built a solid reputation,
you will be rewarded with a sustainable foundation that will work for you.

Other easy strategies include:

- **Business cards**—One of the least expensive forms of
advertising, in my opinion, is through good quality business
cards. This is the first thing you should do when you start
your own business. And don't be afraid to give out business cards! If you are talking to someone who shows even
the slightest interest in your business, give him or her a
card. Slip a handful in the bag with purchases. If you have
brochures, give them out. Keep the information simple,

professional, and readable. Of course, don't forget to mention where you are located and how to contact you!

- **Newsletters**—A monthly or quarterly newsletter can be very effective advertising. A newsletter will be more effective if the content is not obvious advertising but more of a resource. The best approach is not to talk about yourself, but, instead, talk about your customers and offer them unique incentives to purchase. If you have employees, mention any particular skills they bring to the business. Talk about possible gift ideas using your products. Talk about new products you are selling and any specialized services you offer. People who receive your newsletter may pass it on to others.

- **Network**—Networking is a big scary word that simply means talking to people. You have to let people know about your business. Facebook and Twitter will only take you so far; there will come a time when you will have to go offline and meet people. We've all heard the saying, it's not what you know, it's who you know! If you can, wear some of your products, or wear something with your logo on it. Wear bright colors, and you will really stand out among all the others wearing black. When people comment on your business, whip out those business cards. A bit old-fashioned you may think, but it really works! Blake Mycoskie, the founder of Toms Shoes, purposely wears two different pairs of shoes every day so that when people point it out to him he can strike up a conversation with them about his company and its mission.

- **Free listings**—There may be free calendar listings available for certain types of events. If you own a gallery or are hosting any type of event, advertise special exhibitions, performances, or parties by submitting your information to your local newspaper, radio, cable TV, and other media to be included in their community calendar.

PERFECT
YOUR PRODUCT

&

PERFECT
YOUR PITCH!

The right media attention will catapult your business to new levels. But always remember that no amount of marketing and good press will mask a terrible product.

SEVEN PR TIPS TO HELP YOUR BUSINESS SHINE BRIGHT LIKE A DIAMOND

The last thing any entrepreneur wants is to be marked as spam or even blacklisted. The following are some important tips for entrepreneurs dabbling in self-promotion and public relations (PR):

1 Always personalize your pitch. Never copy and paste.
Reporters are known for some unsavory statements regarding pitches that are simply a generic email with the blog name, website, or addressee's name added. I must emphasize the general hatred people have for these irrelevant pitches. Copying and pasting does not give the writer the best angle or story to work with, so you are not utilizing the maximum value of your pitch. A smarter approach is to review the writer's past work and personalize your pitch to something they would write.

2 Determine if your audience and the journalist audience are the same.
Many people have said to me, I would love to be in *Inc. Magazine* or featured on *Entrepreneur Magazine*'s website, but do you have the same audience? Craft a story that's not only similar to one that the journalist would write but one that relates to the overall body of work published by the blog. Cater to what the audience loves. Even if a journalist publishes your story, the effort will be wasted if the audience does not align. If the publication's readers are not engaged, very few will identify with your story. You may receive 5,000 hits without making a sale.

3 Pitch multiple angles of your story.
Segment your media targets, and sell each of them a different angle of your story. Typically, writers are very "vertically" focused, so while your company may work in the mobile, food service, and consumer products areas, make sure your pitch focuses on the writer's area of focus. For example, a pitch to a mobile writer should focus on what you are doing in the mobile space, while a pitch to a consumer-products writer should focus on why the product itself is exciting. Your local paper

would probably like to focus on a human-interest story, such as what you are doing to change your city or town.

4 Smooth talk them without sucking up.

There are genuine ways to be friendly with writers without brown-nosing. Avoid getting involved in their personal lives by asking about friends, family, likes, and dislikes. However, getting involved professionally is simple and ideal. Drop intellectual comments on their blog posts, send an email respectfully criticizing their thoughts, or reply to them with something valuable, such as a clever link or an added thought to one of their tweets.

5 Follow up.

Although some reporters consider this annoying (never follow up several times with the same canned email), this can be a great way to emphasize your enthusiasm about the pitch. Sending a follow-up email saying, "Hey, did you get my last email?" may not be the most effective. However saying something like "I hope you enjoyed my thoughts on our advancements in mobile technology. Here are some new things in mobile tech that are affecting our business and what we are doing to disrupt the industry ...."

6 Join the media.

Become a blogger! Chat with other companies, accept pitches, learn from being on the other side of the table. Becoming a blogger allows you to empathize with other writers. You will receive too many pitches for the limited time you have to write. You will understand why writers prefer to write about some pitches over others. After receiving some terrible pitches, you will realize what makes a good pitch over a bad pitch. You can apply your discoveries to your own PR strategy.

7 It's okay to hook them up....

Never offer to pay a writer a nice sum of money for writing about you, unless you're discussing a sponsored post, which is in a different vein from PR. That's advertising. One way to show a writer love without stuffing his or her pockets with money is to provide a sample product for review. Take note that you should always ask a writer before pushing free products. Some will be offended by free swag that is forced upon them, resulting in wasted product that is tossed in the trash. Writers will typically write about a product sample they like.

Offering a giveaway for the readers is also a great form of bribery. Give the writer something, such as a product or gift card, to offer as a prize to one of their readers. It's a win-win situation all around. You gain exposure, the blog has something new to offer, and the readers can compete for a prize.

WHERE ARE THE MEDIA FEATURE OPPORTUNITIES....

- National TV
- Local TV
- Nationally Syndicated Radio
- Local Radio
- Satellite Radio

- Online Radio
- News Websites
- Blogs
- YouTube Shows
- National Newspapers
- Local Newspapers

QUESTIONS

- Who will pitch stories to the media?
- Who will speak on behalf of your company conducting interviews?
- What makes this person the best fit?
- Do you have high-resolution (hi-res) product photos ready to go?
- How else will you get the word out about your company?
  - Experiential?
  - Sampling strategy?
  - Word of mouth?

Content is KING!

Creating your own blog allows you to constantly put content out in the world, making it easier for journalists to discover you online. Use this worksheet to help you use your social media platforms and blog with the intention of catapulting your brand.

11 TYPES OF STORIES TO PITCH TO THE MEDIA

1. Informative & how-to feature
2. Emerging trends
3. New research
4. Product feature
5. Opinion piece
6. Human interest story
7. Redemption story
8. Employee-to-entrepreneur story
9. Personal profile
10. Expert roundup
11. Local tie-in to national/international story

MEDIA

List the media stories of other businesses that have caught your attention:

1. _____
2. _____
3. _____
4. _____

List the stories (companies not in the same industry) that have caught your attention:

1. _____
2. _____
3. _____
4. _____

Now it's your turn: What are the stories that you can pitch to the media?

1. _____

2. _____

3. _____

4. _____

How to Quickly and Easily Build Your Media List Without Pulling Your Hair Out

Masthead

Every magazine has something called a masthead, which is a list of all the people who were a part of putting the magazine together. You can find it in the first few pages of the magazine. It doesn't usually include the names of freelancers, but you will find everything from the name of the Editor in Chief to the department/beat editors and advertising directors. This will give you the names of the right people to contact and a quick Google search will help you get the contact info of the person you need to reach.

Check Out the Credits

Want to be featured on a TV show? Stop skipping the credits at the end of a show. They're a goldmine! Record the show, and write down the names of the production company and the producer(s), director(s), editor(s), and casting director/casting company. Then check their websites for the contact info, and add it to your pitch list.

Read with Intention

Open up the newspaper you wish to be featured in and look at the stories—in particular, the ones that you would love to have written about you and your company. Then, write down the name of the journalist; these days the contact information usually includes an email address and/or Twitter handle, which makes it soooo easy for you.

Because of the economic downturn, many news outlets rely heavily on freelancers to produce content. Search "Name of Publication + Freelance Writer" to get the name and contact info for freelancers.

BEFORE YOU PITCH TO THE MEDIA, YOU NEED TO HAVE A FEW THINGS READY TO GO AND EASILY AVAILABLE.

Checklist

1. Hi-res product/service imagery photos
2. Hi-res photos of owners
3. Fun bio of owners
4. General press release
5. Two or three angles to pitch to journalist

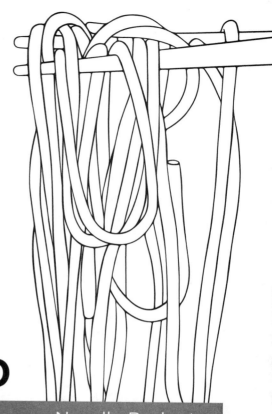

Chapter 10

Social Media on a Ramen Noodle Budget

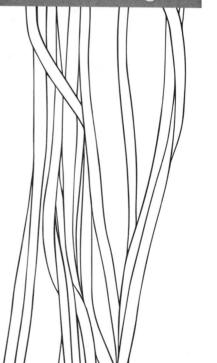

Chapter 10
Social Media on a Ramen Noodle Budget

"Social media requires that business leaders start thinking like small-town shop owners. This means taking the long view and avoiding short-term benchmarks to gauge progress. It means allowing the personality, heart, and soul of the people who run all levels of the business to show."

-Gary Vaynerchuk

Budget

How does a young entrepreneur gain exposure for a new business on a Ramen Noodle budget? Social Media! Consumers have more options than ever in today's market, making it difficult for new businesses to be heard above the noise. Adding to the challenge is the limited marketing budget of most startups. One solution that many entrepreneurs are exploring is social media for promotion. Social media technologies allow people to connect and share things over the internet and offer a way to "level the playing field" of marketing and promotion on a budget. Here, we will explore a number of different social media platforms for promotion, look at case studies of small businesses that have successfully leveraged these tools, and outline a number of strategies for successful social media marketing. Remember, if your company does not have a social media presence it does not exists!

Social Media Platforms

Facebook

Facebook is the most popular social media platform, with a user base and global reach that is unmatched. Facebook provides a lot of opportunities for small businesses to create a social media presence and engage with customers. Entrepreneurs can create pages for businesses, which can be "liked" by Facebook users, allowing users to see updates from the company on their news feed. These updates can serve as a point of engagement between the company and its client base, linking to other pieces of content, such as blog posts, videos, or the company website.

Facebook—Pros and Cons

A major strength of the Facebook platform for promotion is its versatility. You can use a Facebook page to share a variety of messages, using different types of media. This can allow Facebook to serve as the "hub" for your social media marketing efforts—you can easily share all of your marketing content from other media platforms, such as a YouTube video. A big challenge on the Facebook platform is its openness. Because "liking" a business is a relatively public act for a user, visible to all of their friends, it can make users reluctant to do it frivolously, especially for a new business with little exposure. This means that new entrepreneurs have to work very hard to gain traction on their pages by creating relevant content in the form of list, articles, and short videos using Facebook Live to make it easy for people to share with their friends. Facebook has also gotten very crowded, so it's really important to post with intention and add value.

Twitter

Twitter is a very powerful tool for business owners, as it allows companies to share short, timely updates about their enterprise. Entrepreneurs can also share links to longer blog posts or news that is pertinent to their businesses. A big advantage of Twitter is that it levels the playing field of communication, allowing businesses access to influential people and organizations like never before. This makes it a great platform for creating partnerships; getting a re-tweet from an influencer about your business can have a huge marketing impact.

Twitter—Pros and Cons

Because the process of following a Twitter account is more anonymous than a Facebook like, it is often easier to attract followers on Twitter than on Facebook. Twitter updates are often far less involved than Facebook updates. They are simple, with text no longer than 140 characters. It is also well suited for mobile devices, which makes a business Twitter account easy to maintain while tending to the day-to-day needs of your business.

The short nature of the messages, however, can also be a drawback. Twitter updates aren't typically as impactful as messages on other platforms. Most users follow many Twitter accounts and receive individual messages as small touch points in a river of data, making them easily missed or forgotten. In order to stay relevant on Twitter, entrepreneurs need to be constantly updating their accounts, posting regular messages, and monitoring the impact of their message.

YouTube

Video-sharing websites are a potent marketing tool for businesses, and YouTube is the platform of choice.

YouTube has the most users of any video-sharing site; thus, it offers the biggest opportunity for videos to be viewed and shared. Companies can create a branded YouTube channel that features video uploads from the business. And, depending on the copyright usage in the videos, channels can enter into the YouTube partnership program, thereby sharing in the revenue generated by ads that run on the videos.

YouTube—Pros and Cons

YouTube provides a great outlet for providing static content for describing your products or services. A video is worth far more than a thousand words when it comes to providing a business pitch, as users are much more likely to watch a short video than read through pages of text describing your product or business. This makes YouTube a very compelling platform for gaining exposure for physical products. One challenge, however, is that strong, compelling video content can be difficult to produce and can often cost some money. While producing a tweet is quick and free, producing a video that people will want to watch and share may be far harder. This makes YouTube a far higher risk-to-reward proposition than other platforms.

Pinterest

Pinterest is a relative newcomer to the social media scene, but it has grown very quickly in some unique demographics, making it a very powerful tool for certain businesses. While younger males dominate many markets across the Web, Pinterest has attracted an older female user base that may not be as active on other social media.

Pinterest users share photos on pin boards that are organized by themes. These themes tend to center around creative topics, as well as fashion and food.

Pinterest—Pros and Cons

One very powerful advantage of Pinterest is the uniqueness of its user base compared to that of other social media platforms. If you are starting a business that fits well with the themes that dominate Pinterest— food, fashion, or the creative arts—then Pinterest is a great shortcut to reaching your target audience. But Pinterest is not appropriate for all types of business. An internet security firm, for example, would have difficulty getting much traction on the service, as its business isn't consistent with the specific tastes of the user base.

Social Media Success Stories

Many small businesses have used social media platforms to generate exposure and drive business success. Here are three social media success stories and the strategies they employed:

Luxology

Luxology is an independent technology group (acquired by Foundry in 2012) that created a new 3-D software for artists and animators. This is a challenging market to break into, and Luxology decided to use Twitter to promote its new product launch. In order to build excitement for its new "MODO 601" software, Luxology used a promoted account (which means buying low-cost ads on social media) to place tweets on the pages of people who share an interest in 3-D software. This paid option allowed Luxology to speed up its engagement with potential customers. The company also produced video content throughout the day, in response to conversations with customers, on Twitter to stoke the engagement level. By creating new content and engaging with fan conversations, Luxology grew its follower base from 1,700 to nearly 22,000 during this promotion.

Panther Coffee

The Panther Coffee is a Miami-based, independently owned coffee shop. The owners, Joel and Leticia Pollock, relocated from Portland, Oregon, and employed really unique strategies that not only went viral online but also in the streets. Twitter can be a valuable tool even for traditional brick-and-mortar businesses. The married duo started their business in an artists' haven in Miami called Wynwood, where few food and drink options were available. They then brought in a coffee roaster, which enabled them to roast beans on premise. They built a tribe by documenting their roasting process online via Twitter, using very rich photos and videos. They reached out to local customers using the @panthercoffee Twitter account, encouraging people to visit the shop and learn about coffee tasting and cupping. When people visited, the couple would greet each customer and built the relationship by inviting them to live cupping sessions. Soon, loyal customers were placing advance orders using the Twitter account, building the engagement even further. To increase connections, the Pollocks encouraged "Tweet-ups" at the store, so Twitter followers could meet one another and build relationships, which strengthened the following even more. Today, @panthercoffee has over 7,000 followers and is a very active channel for promoting products and events at its various coffee shops.

Blendtec

Blendtec is a great example of a company that used YouTube as a platform to generate business success. Blendtec produces a range of high-powered blenders, a physical product that is a great candidate for a descriptive video to highlight the product's features. However, Blendtec created a product description video with a twist, with the "Will it Blend?" series. The "Will It Blend?" videos featured the Blendtec product blending a series of unusual items, from golf balls to cellphones. The videos went viral, generating over 188 million views for the series. The videos were successful because they provided a unique and interesting piece of content that was short, compelling, and very apt to be shared among friends.

Instead of providing a dry and uninteresting product description, the Blendtec videos provided an exciting talking point that also highlighted the blender's most important differentiating feature: its power.

Vermont County Store

The Vermont County Store is a family-owned "general store" business that expanded into the e-commerce arena and used Facebook very effectively in creating exposure for its online business. In order to increase visits to the company's Facebook wall, the Vermont County Store used sweepstake giveaways to encourage repeat traffic. After incentivizing visits to the page using gift cards and free product giveaways, not only were there more visits, the level of conversation taking place on the page also increased exponentially. This allowed the Vermont County Store to engage with its user base in a much more meaningful way, leading to a large growth in its fan base, to over 30,000 people. The owners then leveraged this following to promote items at the store. They shared personal, yet professional-looking photos that highlighted the rustic nature of the store and area and promoted the differentiating factors of their business.

Social Media Promotion Strategies

These case studies highlight a number of general principles and strategies that you can employ when promoting your business using social media. They include choosing the right platform, giving customers great content, providing incentives to build engagement, monitoring the conversation about your business, showing your humanity and individuality, and finding your target audience. Here's more about each of these important strategies:

Choose a Platform

In today's competitive marketplace, most businesses are operating on almost all social platforms, but you must be careful not to overextend your marketing obligations. It's better to work on fewer platforms and utilize them well than to use all social media outlets and not put enough effort into building a real following. Facebook is the current default choice for social media presence, with Twitter not far behind. Utilize Pinterest or YouTube if your product seems like a good fit for the specific strengths of those services.

Give Customers Great Content

A strong social media strategy starts with great content. Like both Blendtec and Panther Coffee, your messages on social media must be compelling, useful, or entertaining, and they should encourage people to share the message amongst their social network. While many companies simply use social media to speak impassively about their products and services, differentiate your message by making it worth listening to by inviting people into your world, and, most importantly, making it visual with dynamic photos and short videos. Find a way to highlight your product or service features in a way that's entertaining, and always put yourself in the shoes of the customer. Are the pieces of content you're sharing something you would like to receive if you weren't affiliated with the business? Is it something that you would share with your friends? It's difficult to look at your content impartially when you're the owner of the business, but the most effective social media marketers are able to do this and create content that fosters engagement.

Provide Incentives to Build Engagement

As previously mentioned, attracting visitors can be difficult for a new, unknown venture, especially on the Facebook platform. A good way to build an initial fan base is to offer promotions and incentives to keep people visiting your page. Offer a giveaway of your product or service or a personalized experience related to your product, and tie it in with useful content that is shareable. This is one of the areas where you may need to spend some of your limited budget. Building a base of followers on your social media platform is key because these are the people who will start your word-of-mouth marketing message, that is, *if* they decide they like it and want to share it. Give people a compelling reason to keep visiting your page, and eventually habits will form, and customers will integrate your web presence into their daily browsing life. To make a long story short, your site must be interactive! Check out www.Upworthy.com for inspiration on content that is very engaging and sharable.

Monitor Conversations About You

Social media isn't just a platform to allow you to put your message out to the world. When you adopt a social media platform, you also take on the responsibility of monitoring that platform to see how the conversation about your business is taking shape. Search for your business name regularly, and take note of how people are conversing about your product. Identify people who are vocal about your product, and engage with them to ensure they are happy. By monitoring the conversations, you gain valuable data on customer feedback that will allow you to make your product or service better. It's also a great opportunity to offer superb customer service and experiences by identifying any issues and clearing things up. A great customer experience for a client who thinks she's been wronged can be even more valuable than a customer who was satisfied the first time.

Show Your Human Side

One advantage that small business owners have over large corporations in social media is their individuality. At the very core of social media is the formation of human connections, and that rarely happens when interacting with a huge multinational company with thousands of people. Show that you are a real person, and engage with your followers. Like Joel and Leticia from Panther Coffee, interact with your fans on a one-on-one basis, and provide them with meaningful online and offline experiences. The more your customers see you as a real human being, instead of a faceless corporation, the more they'll want to engage with your company.

Find Your Target Audience

As your work on social media progresses, you will start to notice that a few key people will drive the majority of the conversations and social media buzz around your product. In reality, it will be only 10–20% of your user base that will generate up to 80% of the conversations. It's important that you identify these "influencers" early, and bring them to your side to act as evangelists for your product or service. Offer them promotions or advance products so that they create positive buzz and drive the conversations in your favor. Also, use their demographic data to find out information about your typical customer, so you can tailor your marketing message even better.

Steal
from the
Stars

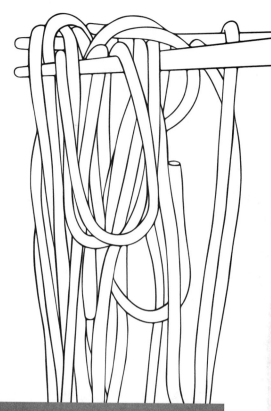

Chapter 11

Steal from the Stars!

Chapter 11
Steal from the Stars!

As much as I wish I could tell you, "If you build it, they will come," I can't. That strategy generally doesn't work for startups when it comes to raising awareness about their business and attracting customers. You need to have a strategic plan to bring in paying clients. In today's digital age, spreading the word about your business is multifaceted; standing out among your competition and being the business that customers pick is a real challenge, but fret not my friends...

There is also another strategy: Stealing tactics and inspiration from celebrities! We can learn a lot from famous people, because becoming famous is ultimately the pinnacle of damn good marketing. So let's see how some of them did it...

Remain
consistent
& true
to your brand!

Success Stories

Nikki Minaj

"You want to know what scares people? Success. When you don't make moves and when you don't climb up the ladder, everybody loves you because you're not competition."

-Nikki Minaj

Entertainers and startup founders have a lot in common. They often find themselves tackling similar marketing dilemmas. Because, at the end of the day, entertainers and CEOs are all trying to connect with an audience, whether it's by using a Groupon deal, Instagram ads, Snapchat videos, hiring sign spinners, or wearing a pink wig to sell out concerts. While I cringe at some of the antics of Nikki Minaj, you can't help notice how she has been able to shake up the music industry in just two short years.

I crowdsourced some of my friends and fellow entrepreneurs on the top 5 marketing lessons young entrepreneurs can learn from Nikki Minaj and other stars, and here's what I learned...

Lesson #1: Remain Consistent and True to Your Brand

She's loud, unique, and a self-glorified Barbie, but it works for her. She markets herself as the Barbie of Hip-Hop/Rap: Taking a beautiful, fashionable, prissy icon and transforming her into a bratty diva, with a monster-esque vernacular! She could have easily switched things up with all the naysayers, but she stayed consistently weird and was able to tap into a unique audience that revels in everything she does. Being true to *yourself* as an entrepreneur will help you tap into an audience that genuinely appreciates you, your work, and your quirkiness.

Lesson #2: Join a Socially Connected Group

I'm not sure if Nikki had labels beating down her door, but she was signed by Young Money Records, a company that was already a big contender in the industry. It's a great lesson in team building. When hiring or building a partnership, look for people that are already socially connected—it's one of the greatest assets you can bring to your company.

Lesson #3: Take an Old Concept and Reinvent It

Sure, we have seen another female rapper do the pink wig thing. It worked to grab our attention then, and it's working for Nikki now. When starting a business, you don't always have to invent or revolutionize an industry. Sometimes, it's as simple as introducing it to a brand new audience. Think of what Rock Band did for 80s rock music sales!

Lesson #4: Individualize a Group Movement

Create a social movement around your brand. With over 3 million followers on Twitter, Nikki Minaj and her marketing team have been very strategic in creating a connection with her audience and allowing them to feel connected emotionally. They've become a part of her "Barbie" cult, similar to Lady Gaga's "Little Monsters" (which I'll talk about a little bit later).

Lesson #5: Make Bold Statements

In the age of social media, if no one is talking about you... then you don't exist. Nikki started with a bold entrance and currently incites a media frenzy everywhere she goes. The hair, the outfits, and the lyrics are crazy, but they all speak very loudly to a very particular audience. Whether you do the crazy hair or wear two different pairs of shoes to strike up conversations about your business (like the owner of Toms Shoes, Blake Mycoskie, did), it doesn't matter—as long as it works for you! It's important to look at other industries or even listen to music to find inspiration to break through the clutter and become a marketing rock star!

Tim Tebow

"It's not about football. It's what we're doing, through faith, hope, and love and the people we serve all over the world. That's going to be bigger than football every single day of my life."

-Tim Tebow

Tim Tebow is best known for his skills as a quarterback—and sometimes for his lack of skills as a quarterback. What many people don't talk about, however, are the skills that make him a phenomenal entrepreneur we can all learn from.

Lesson #1: Remain Consistent and True to Your Brand

We are all aware of the good and not-so-good reviews, rants, and raves about this young man. Yet, what is it that sets him apart from the rest and makes him such a popular athlete? Amidst the harsh analysis and criticisms coming at him from around the globe, he still manages to keep his wits about him as an athlete, a celebrity, and a young professional. Despite many telling him to keep the "Jesus talk" on the down low, Tim Tebow, decided to make it an important part of his life and career. It's a part of who he is; it's his brand. In this fast-paced, cut-throat world, it's hard to find a professional who keeps his cool and remains focused on the goals at hand while not losing sense of his direction or priorities. Tim Tebow consistently delivers a religious, faithful message to his followers—from football lovers to Forbes executives.

Lesson #2: Join a Socially Connected Group

Let's state the obvious: Tim Tebow loves Jesus and isn't afraid to show it. This is what has made him a favorite in the eyes of many Christians. It's given him even more media coverage, because faith-based news stations, media channels, and big name reporters are reaching out to him and supporting him because of the foundation of his faith. While, yes, he's gotten negative media attention from those who claim it to be an act, he has gained more support than negative exposure. For him, it is a genuine devotion and a vital aspect of his career: belief in his faith and religion, believing that it will see him through every avenue and aspect of his success. Without even meaning to, he has connected to Christian, religious, and faith-based groups. It's linked him to conservatives in ways he didn't even intend. By connecting to social groups revolving around faith and God, he has become more popular and successful.

Lesson #3: Take an Old Concept and Reinvent It

The old phrase, "There is no 'I' in Team," comes to mind looking at all that Tim Tebow encompasses as an entrepreneur, a leader, and, of course, an athlete. With his dynamic leadership abilities, refreshing work ethic, and the "it" factor that has everyone talking, Tim Tebow is an influential example of an ideal player not just on the field, but within the workforce as well. Tebow's entire career hinges on his ability to be a key player on his team. Although the focus and attention is directly on Tim Tebow, he consciously disperses this applause and praise amongst his teammates while still holding a heavy amount of responsibility for his team. Business owners and entrepreneurs can learn from this demonstration of teamwork, as a company cannot succeed or thrive unless there is a team attitude that's also being enforced, regardless of how much attention or success a specific employee is receiving.

Lesson #4: Make Bold Statements

Tebow's bold moves—never backing down, speaking for what he believes in, and publicly declaring his faith—simply aren't done anymore. He has made a statement that has many following, admiring, and emulating it in an industry of debauchery, big money, big houses, and even bigger egos.

Lady Gaga

"Some women choose to follow men, and some women choose to follow their dreams. If you're wondering which way to go, remember that your career will never wake up and tell you that it doesn't love you anymore."

-Lady Gaga

Lady Gaga is well known for her phenomenal success within the music industry and for her crazy antics, wacky fashion sense, and strong opinions. What many people don't pay much attention to, however, is how strong her entrepreneurial skills are—skills that have made her one of the most successful female entertainers of this decade.

Lesson #1: Remain Consistent and True to Your Brand

It's hard to get noticed in the entertainment industry, but Lady Gaga knew exactly how to grab the attention of critics, fans, and the rest of the world. We all know her for wearing crazy outfits to every award show, event, and concert, turning heads and leaving people talking for days. When she arrived at the 2010 MTV Awards Show wearing a dress made of meat, Twitter's server overloaded because fans and viewers were in such a frenzy over what she was wearing! Lady Gaga's style is out of this world, and she is not afraid of what other people say or think. She was weird from the beginning and has remained constantly weird.

Lesson #2: Join a Socially Connected Group

Many celebrities support charities, and that gives these charities the ultimate exposure, but Lady Gaga's causes and charities are especially close to her heart. She was bullied as a kid and into her young adulthood years for her appearance and unique ways, along with her sexuality and passionate support for the LGBT community. Lady Gaga used her passion and emotional ties to reach out to these groups of people and formed tight ties with the organizations and fans ready to support them. Even though these causes and organizations are close to Gaga's heart, it's a fantastic strategy as people are more likely to purchase an item or join a cause if their favorite pop idol or celebrity supports it, too.

Lesson #3: Individualize a Group Movement

Lady Gaga's popularity went viral through videos, interviews, and interaction with her fan base, all of which drove her social media success. Her online impact through video channels allowed her to create a group movement and a community called *Little Monsters*, fans of all races, sexual orientations, sizes, and backgrounds have connected with her through this—and with one another.

She's a spokesperson for YouTube, Google+, and Google Chrome because of her ability to create a campaign about connecting with others around the world regardless of background or orientation. Her movement was created through online marketing. One does not need to pour funds and resources into online marketing, it is simply done by spreading the word to a fan base, through social media and creative videos. Lady Gaga took advantage of YouTube from the very beginning of her career, posting and receiving over a million hits on many of her videos. This is an example to all entrepreneurs of the effectiveness of creative videos, viral marketing, and utilizing social media networking.

Take an
old concept and

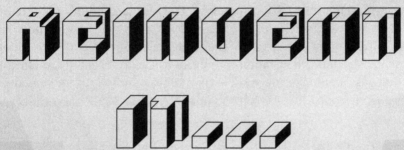

IT...

Lesson #5: Make Bold Statements

Gaga continues to brand herself as an eccentric artist who always leaves us wondering, "What's next?" She must be doing something right, as she remains one of the most highlighted and talked about artists in the industry. Lady Gaga's record sales have hit chart-topping numbers over the past years. She has set records and made history, and she has set the stage as a successful businesswoman whom all professionals and entrepreneurs should learn from.

Jeremy Lin

"A perfect plan doesn't mean that it ends up the way that you want it to end up. You don't get better if you win all the time, you get better when you lose, you improve when you lose"

-Jeremy Lin

We know of Jeremy Lin (Jeremy Shu-How Lin) as a professional basketball player, first for the New York Knicks and then for the Charlotte Hornets. The NBA All Star has made history, made news, and made a name for himself far sooner and quicker than he ever thought imaginable.

Lesson #1: Remain Consistent and True to Your Brand

This basketball star does not fit your typical mold at all. Jeremy Lin is a Harvard graduate in economics and is of Asian descent. These unique factors, along with his exceptional talent, are what have made Jeremy rise above the NBA crowd. Jeremy's "it" factor has also made him desirable among partners and other companies looking for celebrity endorsements and affiliations. Volvo hired him to be their spokesperson in order to enhance its cars' brand awareness and popularity. Jeremy Lin's story is one that displays to professionals and entrepreneurs looking to succeed that good things can happen to those who wait and work extremely hard for their goals and dreams to become reality. Jeremy Lin's positive attributes and strong suits are not necessarily the typical qualities you might find in an NBA player's story: Asian Harvard grad who came off the bench and led his team to victory. However, Jeremy Lin's ability to stand out in the crowd in a highly competitive career is what makes him an even a greater leader and athlete to emulate.

Lesson #2: Join a Socially Connected Group

Jeremy Lin hasn't just connected with one specific group, but his personality and career resonates well with people of all ages and around the world. An athlete who is able to connect with more than one social group, just as Jeremy Lin does, is a diamond in the rough. One of the things that so many people notice when Jeremy Lin takes the court is that he is one of the few who keep smiling. Countless photos, snapshots, and game highlights show this athlete bearing a big grin—something we do not see that often in a world of high-intensity and ever-competitive sports. It is through this that we can look to emulate Jeremy's way of life—live life to its fullest, enjoy the ride, and smile through it all.

Jeremy Lin's positive attitude shows through in everything he does. In every commercial, partnership, press conference, and interview, Jeremy expresses his joy in his career and all that it entails. He acknowledges the fact that getting to where he is in his basketball journey required hard work, dedication, and persistence, but every moment of it has been worth it. This is an excellent lesson to all entrepreneurs as they push for what they want and as they yearn to succeed and make their mark within the professional world.

Lesson #3: Take an Old Concept and Reinvent It

Jeremy reinvented what it means to be a team member. We all hear the various sayings regarding being a team player, but few follow it on and off the court. Any athlete knows the importance of being a team player and all that it entails. Jeremy Lin is a loyal member of the Charlotte Hornets and acts as a team member on and off the court. He never speaks an ill word about anyone on the team, past or present, and represents himself in a way that only paints the Hornets in a positive light.

Any business professional or entrepreneur knows how important it is to have the "best of the best" on their team. Bringing on the shining stars of the public relations, marketing, and business world and adding them to your team is the best thing you can do for everyone involved. The phrase "there is no I in team" must be carried out by each member of your team, in and out of the office, just as Jeremy Lin does for his team. He is a key team member and player, and his positive behavior as a member of his team continues to bring them much success.

Lesson #4: Individualize a Group Movement

"Linsanity" is the phrase heard around the world when people hear Jeremy Lin's name. Linsanity is the phenomenon that made Jeremy Lin so famous and stand out amongst others in the NBA. This began when Jeremy Lin made his team undefeated champions. It was one win after another, one success after another, and continued success that kept Jeremy Lin humble but ever so confident. Jeremy Lin has created his success to be a science, and sports psychologists would study his success, mindset, and agenda as he continued to succeed in his career. He is able to block out outside pressure, negativity, and distractions. Linsanity took off around the world as Jeremy Lin began to campaign, speak to teens and young adults, and encourage them. After each success and win, Jeremy wouldn't just give credit to himself. Instead, he gave credit to his team, God, and his fans who kept believing in him and in the "Linsanity" of his jaw-dropping career.

Lesson #5: Make Bold Statements

Nobody expected this tall, lanky, Harvard grad of Asian descent to make history and become a basketball legend. By maintaining confidence in his culture, it reminded the world that we should not put people in boxes based on their ethnicity. What was even more unexpected is that he turned down numerous endorsement deals in the beginning in order to focus just on playing basketball. Nevertheless, Jeremy Lin went against all odds and assumptions about who he could be and surpassed any expectations, and he's a worldwide phenomenon because of it. Companies are constantly looking to have him endorse major multi-million dollar products and campaigns, he has fans all over the world, and he continues to make NBA history.

Enjoying your career, creating a positive reputation for yourself, and maintaining a key team player attitude throughout your business endeavors are key factors to succeeding in the world of business, marketing, and finance. Jeremy Lin demonstrates these qualities on and off the court, which is what makes him such an influential celebrity, athlete, and model for every entrepreneur looking to succeed.

MAKE
BOLD
STATEMENTS

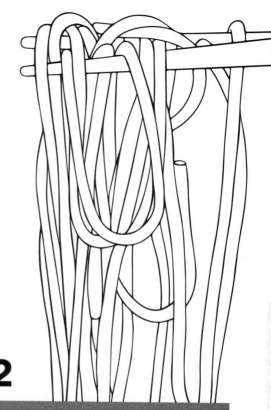

Chapter 12

Do Epic Shit

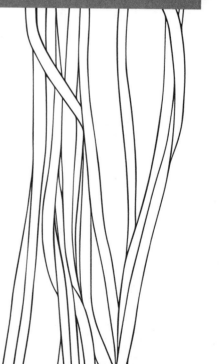

Chapter 12
Do Epic Shit

As you are building your business on a Ramen Noodle budget, you will have to overcome many obstacles as you commit yourself to steady, organic growth. I want to close out this book sharing some tips on how to stay motivated on your journey. Remember, you are not cooking up a microwave meal. This is a journey. You are taking your idea and turning it into a business—a 7-course gourmet meal—and along the way pots will burn, things will boil over, and you will have to cook for different tastes, all while keeping focused on preparing a dish that will look good and taste good. And, as your business grows, it will create amazing revenue that will allow you to not just eat, but feast.

But you must stay hungry, hungry for every opportunity to build a business that will be epic. And when you are on stage speaking to thousands of people to share your story, you will tell them that you started on a Ramen Noodle budget or as Drake says "You started from the bottom and now you are here"

Follow Your Passion Blah, Blah, Blah

You hear it all the time: Follow Your Passion and you will never feel like you are working a day in your life ... Right!!!? Um, news flash: It does and will feel like work, and, as an entrepreneur, you can't take "passion" to the bank and try to cash it. (I'm pretty sure I unsuccessfully tried that a few years ago!)

You will work harder than you have ever in your life, but it will be the most rewarding work of your life when you truly live out your passion.

When you are truly, truly aligned with your passion, it will not feel like work because you will be aligned! But I've found that passion really comes into play in those tough dark moments when obstacles are in your way, and those obstacles feel so big that they could swallow you. When you feel like nothing is left, *passion* is that little voice deep down in the pit of your stomach that tells you to click into overdrive, and it continues to whispers...follow me!

How to Stay Focused During the Rollercoaster of Entrepreneurship:

1 **Create your Epic Shit List.**
Sometimes, we just need a trip down good old memory lane. In this list, you will include anything and everything that you have ever accomplished—from your little league trophy to positive feedback from your old boss, clients, customers, family, friends, and strangers. I've created a template for you to Collect all Your Epicness and visit whenever you are feeling like an impostor. (I find it best to create this list when you are having a freaking fantastic day, when you're feeling the most like yourself. For whatever reason, you tend to dig deeper.) Visit www.Feleciahatcher.com/freedownload to get your free "Epic Shit List" worksheet.

2 **Identify your "Are you Kidding Me" friend.**
You know those friends who allow you to vent, but then immediately say, "Are you kidding me? Do you know how much you have accomplished?" Aside from my husband Derick, I have two great friends, James Taylor with Taylored Athletes and Casandra Henriquez with Inspire Many who provide that dose of reality.

3 **Stay in your own lane.**
I find that the times I feel the most intimidated is when I start venturing into lanes that are not my own. I'm not saying don't take risks and don't try new things. But realize what you are extremely good at and what you truly suck at. Because there are

times in the impostor syndrome when you truly are being a greedy impostor instead of being honest and acknowledging when you can use some help. If you don't know something, don't think Google will save you. Admit that you don't know, but realize that you do know someone who does and put that person on it. As I always say, "the pie is big enough for everyone to get a slice."

4 Curse.
So, I'm known to have a motivational potty mouth, and I happily accept this. Sometimes, the only way to motivate yourself to really get out of a rut, to really unleash your badassery is to, well, put a little *stank* on it. Because you got this, I mean, you really *f**king* got this!

5 Stop letting Luck steal the credit for your hard work.
You worked your ass off for this! Everything you have done leading up to that point, every late night, every proposal, every pitch, all the NOs, and every yes. Every sacrifice, every struggle, every epic failure, and every success has led to that moment. It is not Luck! You deserved that opportunity, you deserve to be in that room, and you deserve a seat at the table—unapologetically accept it! You are not selling snake oil. You are creating a company, working on a project, or starting a movement that is going to have a huge impact on the world, and it takes time. And, yes, you don't know all the answers, but you do know your stuff, so stop playing small and thinking small so that others can feel big. Because if everyone were more honest about the process, you would see that we have all jumped off the mountain and are building a plane and trying to fly all at the same time. You are not an impostor. You, my dear, are GRINDING!

6 Watch my favorite YouTube video that I watch when I'm feeling down during the entrepreneurial journey.
There's a video on YouTube featuring Michael Jordan, where he says that maybe he made things look too easy for every

basketball player who came after him. It's an old video, but it has meaning far beyond basketball. As a business owner, I have had to overcome many challenges, and a few times, I strongly considered throwing in the towel with Feverish because it got too hard, and I knew I could easily earn money and would not have to work so hard going back to a 9-to-5 marketing job. I'll be the first to tell you that owning a business is the hardest but most rewarding experience of my life. You will never be able to build true generational wealth working for someone else.

When I first started, I underestimated the amount of sacrifice that it takes to own a business and follow a dream. MJ's video really made me stop in my tracks. Here is a transcript of it:

Michael Jordan Video Transcript

Maybe it's my fault.

Maybe I let you to believe it was easy, when it wasn't.

Maybe I made you think my highlights started at the free-throw line, and not at the gym.

Maybe I made you think that every shot I took was a game winner. That my game was built on flash, and not fire.

Maybe it's my fault that you didn't see that failure gave me strength. That my pain was my motivation.

Maybe I led you to believe that basketball was a God-given gift, and not something I worked for every single day of my life.

Maybe I destroyed the game.

Or maybe, you're just making excuses.
Become legendary.

Closing Thoughts...

I want to leave you with some final words. I usually like to live by this quote "Celebrate your success, for you and only you know your struggles."

We often see people in places and wish that we could have what they have or be where they are, but the words *sacrifice* and *struggle* both come before the word *success* in the dictionary. Sure, they are ugly words! Heck, I despise them at times, but I've learned that no matter how much talent and luck you have, you still have to work hard. The people we currently look up to, they make it look easy. Too often magazines, movies, and society in general want to paint the picture of the overnight success.

Michael Jordan made every free throw, slam-dunk, and ankle-breaking crossover look so damn effortless, but he made it to where he was one shot at a time, with lots of failures along the way. With great risk comes great reward, but you will never see the reward if you don't take the first step!

Fear is the main reason we don't become successful, so I challenge you after reading this book to...

Get super creative and start your business on a Ramen Noodle budget!

Look beyond your limits and rise to your potential.

Don't be afraid of staying up until 5 a.m. working on your idea only to wake back up at 7 a.m. because you have to work a 9-to-5 full-time job.

Don't be afraid if your bank account hit $0 because you needed to buy that extra foot of fabric to make a mock-up to pitch to a potential client.

Don't be afraid to sleep in your car for 6 months, because you believe so much in your screenplay you used all your money to drive to Los Angeles.

Don't be afraid to get that pink slip, because you have been daydreaming for two years about leaving to start your own marketing company.

Don't be afraid to quit your "safe" job because your dreams are so much bigger than your cubicle. Honestly, with the way the economy is, no job is safe!

Don't just strive to be successful—become legendary!

And, my personal favorite:

Do Epic Shit

About the Author

Felecia Hatcher-Pearson is a White House Award-winning entrepreneur, badass business rainmaker, bestselling author, globally sought-after speaker, media darling, mother, and co-founder of Code Fever and BlackTechWeek. Breathe. She is also the rather awesome former Chief Popsicle at Feverish Pops, a gourmet ice pop boutique and manufacturing brand with a Fortune 500 client roster that would make your head spin.

For the past decade, Felecia has dedicated her life to inspiring a new generation of leaders to DO EPIC SHIT, through her conversational talks on Entrepreneurship, Tech Innovation, Funding, and Personal Branding. As the founder of Code Fever and Black Tech Week, Felecia has spearheaded the movement of the Miami Startup ecosystem focused on getting marginalized individuals to become major players in the innovation economy.

Hatcher has been featured on MSNBC, NBC's *Today Show*, The Cooking Channel, *Essence Magazine*, *Entrepreneur*, BET, Black Enterprise, and the *Miami Herald*.

So ...

Let's work together and astonish the world!

WWW.FELECIAHATCHER.COM

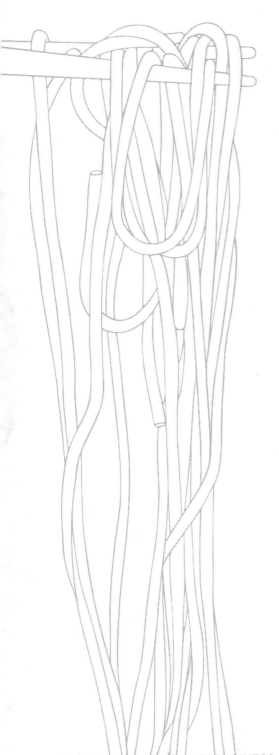

NOTES & IDEAS FOR *MY* BUSINESS ON A RAMEN NOODLE BUDGET